ONE HUNDRED
BREAD
MACHINE
RECIPES

ONE HUNDRED
BREAD
MACHINE
RECIPES

VICKI SMALLWOOD

ISLAND BOOKS

This edition published in 2002 by
S. WEBB & SON (Distributors) LTD
Telford Place, Pentraeth Road, Menai Bridge,
Isle of Anglesey, LL59 5RW

© 2002 D&S Books Ltd

D&S Books
Cottage Meadow, Bocombe,
Parkham, Bideford
Devon, England
EX39 5PH

e-mail us at:-
enquiries@dsbooks.fsnet.co.uk

This edition printed 2002

ISBN 1-85605-713-5

Creative Director: Sarah King
Editor: Clare Haworth-Maden
Project editor: Sally MacEachern
Photographer: Colin Bowling/Paul Forrester/Laura Forrester
Designer: Dave Jones

Typeset in Galliard and Helvetica

Printed in China

1 3 5 7 9 10 8 6 4 2

CONTENTS

INTRODUCTION

BREAD HAS BEEN A BASIC STAPLE OF OUR DIETS for thousands of years, and nearly every nationality has a particular type of bread for which it is known: the French have the baguette, for instance, the Mexicans the tortilla, the Italians the focaccia, the Germans rye bread, the Americans corn bread, the Punjabis the naan, and so on. And although the ready sliced loaf may have firmly established itself in Western society, people will often go out of their way to enjoy a freshly baked loaf. When reminiscing about the food that they ate, one of the things that is often mentioned time and again by people who have spent their holidays in France, is the fine bread that they had, by which you can be sure that they don't mean a ready sliced loaf. In France, bread-making remains an institution that is treated with the reverence that it deserves.

Coming into a room and smelling the aroma of freshly baked bread is enough to tempt and welcome anyone, and there is no better accompaniment to a meal than a freshly baked loaf. Bread is so versatile that it can be the main feature of a meal, a tasty addition or one of the easiest, most wholesome snacks that it is possible to put together. A nutritionally valuable food, bread provides us with protein, calcium, iron, thiamine (vitamin B1) and niacin, making it an important part of our daily diet. It is a basic part of our everyday lives, and no matter which foods are currently vogue, some form of bread will always accompany them. The flavours, shape or style of the bread may change, but its basis of flour, water and yeast will always stay the same.

We may sadly have lost many of our local bakers, but with the help of a bread machine and a handful of ingredients, you could soon be supplying your family with wholesome, good-quality, nutritious loaves, with far less effort than it takes to drive to the supermarket. If you prefer organic produce, the range of organic ingredients that is increasingly available makes it easy to make your own organic bread at home. And with the many and varied recipes in this book, you will be stuck for choice as to which type of bread to make.

Until recently, the most expensive ingredient involved in the making of a loaf of bread was time. Now, however, the ready availability and ease of use of domestic bread machines means that this is no longer the case. Even the most basic model gives you a selection of programmes that will enable you either to make a loaf from start to finish or else to produce dough that you can finish yourself by hand and using a conventional cooking method. As well as being widely available, bread machines are now sold in varying sizes, and the only restriction that one will place upon you is the size of the loaf or piece of dough that you can make – only a minor argument against investing in one. The model that was used to make the loaves in this book has the capacity to produce a finished loaf weighing 1100g (about 2½lb).

An example of one of the many bread machines on the market. This model can carry out two separate functions at the same time

If you love freshly baked bread, it won't be long after buying a bread machine that you'll be wondering how you got by without it. As long as you have the right ingredients and the time to measure them and place them in the baking pan, making delicious bread could not be easier. So straightforward are bread machines to use, that coming downstairs to tuck into a freshly baked loaf for breakfast will simply require measuring your ingredients the day before and setting the timer – how simple is that? There is also  something incredibly satisfying about watching the food that you have made being eaten and enjoyed by your loved ones. Bread machines are capable of doing more than producing a finished loaf, too: you can also use them to make cakes, marmalades and jams.

Because it'll be additive- and preservative-free, the bread that you've made with your bread machine may not last as long as shop-bought bread, but when the aroma of a warm loaf is wafting through the house, you'll be lucky to have any left in any case, while freshly made bread that has dried out a little makes perfect toast.

Tips for success

As with all baking, bread-making is an exact science. The ingredients need to be used in the right proportions and under the correct conditions in order to create the required result. Reading and absorbing the following tips should help you to create your own tasty loaves time after time.

1 I recommend that you first follow a few of the recipes that the manufacturer has supplied with your bread machine so that you become used to the method that your machine requires. It is especially crucial to add the ingredients in the order that is appropriate for your machine, but once you have become used to that, any bread-machine recipe can be adapted to work in your machine. When following any of the recipes in this book, remember that your bread-machine's capacity needs to be equal to a loaf weighing 1100g (about 2½lb).

2 Always measure your ingredients accurately. When using a cup or spoon, remember that the ingredient being measured should be level with the top of the utensil and not heaped above it. (Similarly, ingredients should neither be packed nor pressed down into the cup or spoon.) To level off the ingredient in a cup or spoon, take a knife and run it across the top to remove any excess.

Measuring cups   Measuring spoons   Measuring jug

3 Unless otherwise stated, your ingredients should be at room temperature. Ingredients that are too cold will hinder the working power of the yeast, while too much heat will kill it off. Liquids should be tepid, and a quick and easy way of judging whether they are is to dip your finger into them: if the liquid feels warm, but not hot, it is just right (it's a bit like testing a baby's bathwater).

4 When preparing your ingredients, always ensure that the yeast does not come into contact with any liquid, which would activate the yeast prior to the correct time and thus spoil the end result. If the instructions that have come with your bread machine specify that the yeast should be added last, place the flour in the baking pan, make a small indentation in the top and then spoon the yeast into

it. This will keep the yeast particles both together and dry by preventing any stray granules from rolling down the sides of the flour into the liquid. At this point, it is also advisable to keep any salt away from the yeast.

5 While it is being mixed, it's a good idea to check the dough because the prevailing climate and temperature can both have an effect on it. The dough ingredients should come together in what looks like a smooth ball that is slightly springy to the touch. If the dough is looking too wet, add a little extra flour (one tablespoon at a time). If it is looking too dry, a little tepid water may be needed, again added in small amounts to avoid making the dough too wet. If some of the ingredients have caught at the sides of the baking pan, take a rubber spatula and carefully incorporate them into the dough as quickly as possible.

6 If you are intending to leave the machine on its timer, it is best not to do so if the recipe requires fresh ingredients like eggs, cream, buttermilk or fresh milk because they may spoil. It's preferable instead to use a recipe that does not include fresh ingredients, although using dried milk is fine.

The best bread-making ingredients

FLOUR

When shopping for flour to use in your bread machine, always look for a flour that is labelled 'strong' or 'bread' flour (some millers are now producing flour that is labelled as being perfect for use in bread machines). Many supermarkets and high-street shops stock various types of bread-making flour, and the more unusual ones can generally be bought from good health-food shops.

Self-raising or plain flour simply will not do because both are 'soft' flours, meaning that they do not have a high enough gluten content.

13

Similarly, gluten-free flours are also unsuitable when it come to making bread. By contrast, 'strong' or 'bread' flours are particularly high in the gluten that is essential to produce the correct texture for loaves of bread. Brown and wholemeal flours generally produce a denser, smaller loaf than when white flour is used.

Flour is best stored in a cool, dry, dark place, in the bag in which it was bought (if the bag is torn, transfer the flour to a plastic food bag). As with all ingredients, check the flour's sell- or use-by date before using it. If it is out of date, or you are in doubt about it, discard it and buy some fresh flour. If your bag of flour has been left unused for some time, it may have become compressed, thus preventing you from obtaining a correct cup measurement, so gently stir the flour around before measuring it out.

SALT

Salt is an essential ingredient that is not only used to bring out the flavour of the bread, but also to control the growth of the yeast, which is why you should not adjust the recommended quantity – even for dietary reasons – because it may affect your finished loaf. Salt also plays a part in causing the crust to change colour during the baking process.

SUGAR

Sugar speeds up the action of the yeast, as well as having a softening effect on the gluten in the flour, which is why rich, sweet breads generally have a closer texture. While not all bread doughs require sugar, adding it will make the bread-making process faster, although note that adding too much sugar will inhibit the yeast's action.

Generally speaking, you should use a sugar that dissolves easily, which is why I recommend using either caster sugar or runny honey (set honey is not suitable). Using golden caster sugar instead of the standard white will make no difference because it is the sugar's dissolving quality, rather than its colour, that is important. Depending on the variety that you use, honey can impart a flavour of its own, so why not experiment with your favourite varieties? Honey also contains fewer calories than sugar, which is something to bear in mind if you are counting the calories. If you aren't fond of honey, you could use golden syrup instead, while treacle offers alternative colouring, flavouring and sweetening qualities. Never use artificial sweeteners, however, because they will not react with the yeast.

YEAST

Yeast is the raising agent in bread-making: once activated, it creates carbon dioxide, small bubbles of which become trapped within the gluten-rich dough, and it is the carbon dioxide that the yeast creates that gives bread its characteristic texture. Contrary to popular belief, yeast can withstand the cold, so should you wish to make your dough

the night before baking it and then store it in the fridge, it will continue to rise overnight, just more slowly than at room temperature. If you do this, it is best to allow the dough to return to room temperature before finishing the proving process (see page 20) and baking it.

The recipes in this book use a dried yeast that is suitable for bread-makers, which you should find in any good supermarket. Not only will the result be inferior if you use fresh yeast, but dried yeast is far more convenient. As long as you store it properly, it will last for several months and will thus be on hand for any loaf of bread that you decide to bake on the spur of the moment.

Yeast needs to be stored in a cool, dry place, preferably the fridge. A half-used tin of yeast will keep better if it is placed in a smaller container because coming into contact with air will cause it to deteriorate. Make sure that you reseal the lid properly after using dried yeast, always store it according to the manufacturer's instructions and make sure that you check the expiry date each time that you use it (stale yeast is a common reason why bread does not rise properly).

If in doubt regarding the freshness of your yeast, sprinkle half a teaspoon of caster sugar into half a cup of tepid water and stir the mixture until the sugar has dissolved. Now sprinkle one teaspoon of the yeast over the surface, cover the cup with a piece of clingfilm and leave it in a warm place for ten minutes. When you return to inspect it, the liquid should have a foamy head and smell quite yeasty. If this is not the case, the yeast is no longer active and you need to buy a fresh supply.

BICARBONATE OF SODA (BAKING SODA) AND BAKING POWDER

Bicarbonate of soda (baking soda) and baking powder are the raising agents used in quick breads (which have more of a cake-like texture than other breads), which require an alternative raising agent because they do not contain yeast.

LIQUIDS

Water is the liquid that is most commonly used in bread-making, although milk, fruit juice and beer can also be used.

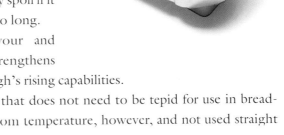

Milk adds nutritional value to a loaf, as well as improving its keeping quality and the colour of its crust. If you are using a delayed-time programme, I recommend that you use dried skimmed milk with the appropriate volume of water rather than whole milk, which may spoil if it is left in the machine for too long.

Fruit juice adds flavour and colour to a loaf and also strengthens the gluten, aiding the dough's rising capabilities.

Beer is the only liquid that does not need to be tepid for use in bread-making; it should be at room temperature, however, and not used straight from the fridge.

EGGS

Whole eggs or egg yolks add a lovely texture and richness to your loaf. Do not, however, use recipes that require eggs when you are intending to leave the bread machine on its timer because they may spoil.

OILS AND FATS

Oils and fats add a quality of their own to a loaf by improving its texture and enriching its flavour.

I recommend using butter that has been melted and cooled, although you could alternatively use very soft butter, the most important thing being that it must not be hot and must blend with the other ingredients easily. Margarine is equally suitable, and has the added benefit of being an unsaturated fat. If you wish to substitute oil for margarine or butter you may do so, and oil is generally more subtle in flavour than butter, which tastes very rich.

The bread-making process

This section explains the process that your bread-making machine will go through while making your bread or dough

MIXING THE INGREDIENTS

Once you have set the programme to the desired cycle and have pressed the start button, some machines will remain suspiciously quiet. Don't be alarmed: if you look at the timer, you'll see that the minutes are indeed ticking away, showing that your machine is working. What is happening is that it is gently warming the ingredients to the correct temperature (this may not have been explained very clearly in the manufacturer's manual), after which the mixing process will begin.

KNEADING THE DOUGH

When the mixing process has been completed, the kneading stage will begin. A few minutes before the kneading process has been completed, a bleep will indicate that you should add any outstanding ingredients. This is the time to add any ingredients that may otherwise have been damaged during the mixing stage, such as dried fruits or nuts.

THE FIRST RISING

The machine will automatically complete the first rising for you, and if you are only making dough, it will then bleep to indicate that the cycle is complete.

KNOCKING BACK, OR THE SECOND KNEADING

If you have set your machine to 'BASIC', it will complete the knocking-back process for you. If, however, you specified the 'DOUGH' programme, this is the point at which you should take over and finish the bread-making process by hand. The steps that follow, your machine will automatically perform if set to BASIC. However if finishing by hand, you will need to be familiar with these terms. Knocking back is the term that is used when you literally knock the risen dough back down again. It only takes a couple of minutes and should be done on a lightly floured surface.

RESTING THE DOUGH

The dough sometimes needs to rest briefly between the knocking-back and shaping processes, particularly if it is a little too springy. If this is the case, once the dough has been kneaded, loosely cover it and leave it for five to ten minutes before proceeding

SHAPING THE DOUGH

How to shape the dough is explained fully in the individual recipes. As you gain experience and confidence, however, you can please yourself and try experimenting.

PROVING THE DOUGH

Proving is the term that is used when the dough rises for the second, and final, time, during which stage it should be left in a warm, draught-free place until it has almost doubled in size. (It is important not to allow the dough to rise too much because it may then collapse; if this happens, remove the dough, knead it again and then return it to prove once more.)

While it is proving, the dough should be covered to ensure that its surface doesn't dry out. The best way of doing this is loosely covering it with either a piece of lightly oiled clingfilm or a damp and clean, or a lightly floured and

clean, tea towel, allowing the dough plenty of room within which to rise. A large polythene food bag that has had a couple of drops of oil rubbed over the inside is also extremely effective.

In many cases, the slower the proving process, the better the texture of the finished loaf.

The temperature within the machine is programmed to provide perfect rising and proving conditions.

FINISHING THE BREAD

Although the recipes for some of the hand-finished breads in this book specify a glaze or finish, you can also add a glaze or finish to entirely machine-baked breads or experiment to suit your preferences. Here are some finishing ideas.

For a crisp, shiny loaf, brush the top with a little beaten egg. Although this is usually done before the loaf is baked, if you want to give a machine-baked loaf this finish, you will need to place it in a hot oven for five minutes to cook off the egg and fix the glaze. If you

wish, before baking the loaf, you could sprinkle a tablespoon or so of your favourite seeds or chopped nuts over it.

Brushing a finished loaf with a little milk will result in a softer crust.

Sweet breads may be brushed with a half-and-half mixture of sieved apricot jam and warmed water, a procedure that needs no further cooking and results in a shiny, slightly sticky, finish.

Brushing a loaf with a fifty-fifty mixture of caster sugar dissolved in warm milk will give a high sheen and will slightly soften the crust.

BAKING HAND-FINISHED DOUGH

Once the dough has been proved, it must go into a hot oven to enable the heat to kill the yeast and the bread to be cooked.

If you like a particularly crusty finish to your bread, try to introduce some steam to the oven, which will also encourage the bread to rise evenly. To do this, fill a clean plant spray with water and, when you are about to put the loaf into the oven to bake, spray a little water into the oven, avoiding any gas jets or heating elements as far as you can, before placing the loaf in the oven. Spray the inside of the oven again five minutes later, opening and closing the door as quickly as you can to avoid causing too much heat loss. If the top of the loaf looks as though it is burning without being cooked through, cover it with a piece of tin foil and continue to bake the bread.

At the end of the baking time, if you tap it with your knuckle and it sounds hollow, the bread will be cooked through. Alternatively, test it by inserting a skewer into the centre of the loaf; if it comes out clean, that is, with no moist dough sticking to it, the loaf is ready.

Problems and solutions

If you find that your finished loaf does not look as perfect as you had hoped, don't despair: such 'interesting-looking' loaves are still good to eat. Take it as a sign that you either need to make a few adjustments or else take greater care when adding and measuring ingredients the next time you make it.

Checking the dough as it is being mixed can sometimes make all the difference to a loaf because it enables you to judge whether the dough is too wet or dry (see page 12). Although you can correct the texture of the dough in this way, you can't judge whether it contains too much – or too little – salt or yeast, so it's important to measure your ingredients carefully and not to leave any out.

Here are some solutions to a number of common bread-making problems.

The bread did not rise enough

If the bread did not rise enough, the cause could be one of several things. First check that your yeast was not out of date and also that it was still active (see page 16 for the testing method).

Other causes could have been adding too little sugar or yeast or too much salt, which is why you should always measure your ingredients accurately.

Ask yourself, too, whether the yeast could have been activated before the cycle started. If you suspect this to have been the case, remember to make sure that the yeast does not come into contact with any liquid in the baking pan.

Finally, if any liquid was too hot, it could have killed the yeast, so ensure that liquids measure between 21 and 28°C on the temperature scale unless otherwise specified.

The bread has sunk in the centre

If the bread has sunk in the centre, this may have been caused by the inclusion of too much liquid (as ever, remember to measure the ingredients accurately) or of ingredients that either weren't drained properly or were simply too wet. (This can sometimes happen with cheese breads because each type of cheese has a different moisture content.) As long as the bread has cooked through, however, it will still taste fine.

To solve this problem, try reducing the liquid content a little, as well as thoroughly draining any canned or fresh fruit or vegetables and blotting them dry with kitchen paper.

Because a lack of salt can also cause bread to sink in the centre (it will rise too much, subsequently causing it to collapse), remember to add salt.

High altitudes or humidity can have an effect on the finished loaf, too, so if you live at a high altitude or in an area of high humidity, you may need to reduce the amount of yeast that you include by quarter of a teaspoon.

The crust is damp and lost its crunch

A damp crust is generally caused by not promptly transferring the bread to a wire rack at the end of the baking cycle, as a result of which condensation forms, making the loaf wet.

To rectify a damp crust, cook the loaf in a hot oven for a few minutes, then remove it from the oven and leave to cool on a wire rack before serving it.

The centre is soggy and uncooked

To avoid a loaf having a soggy centre, always drain fresh or canned fruit or vegetables well. Alternatively, try reducing the liquid content a little.

The bread rises too much

If the bread rises too much, this can usually be put down to inaccurate measuring: too much flour or yeast, too little salt, or liquid that is too warm can all play a part in creating this problem.

If you live in an area of high humidity, you may find it best to bake your bread during the coolest part of the day, not to use the timer function and to use liquids straight from the fridge.

Storing your bread

Once the bread has been cooled on a wire rack, you should store it ready for use. It is best to store bread in a container in order to retain its moisture content, thereby keeping it fresher for longer. Wrapping bread in clingfilm is not advisable because this can encourage the formation of mould.

FREEZING YOUR BREAD

All of the breads included in this book are suitable for freezing. If the finished loaf, roll or bun requires icing, however, do this after you have defrosted the bread because icing or sugary toppings do not freeze well and will affect the quality of the finished item.

To freeze your baked bread, wrap it either in some freezer-proof foil or a freezer bag, removing as much air as possible in the process. Then clearly label the packaging with the date when the bread was made, as well as its name, because after a week or so you'll probably have forgotten these details.

In general, most types of bread are best used within three months. Remember to defrost the bread completely at room temperature before serving it.

USING UP STALE SCRAPS

Bread is ever versatile, and if you have some stale scraps left over, you can put them to good use by turning them into breadcrumbs. Break the scraps into pieces and whiz them in a blender or food processor. Breadcrumbs are ideal for mixing with cheese and sprinkling over a pasta or vegetable dish, which you could then flash under the grill or briefly brown in a hot oven. For variety, add some chopped nuts or fresh herbs. Alternatively, use freshly made breadcrumbs in any dish that calls for them.

If you are not planning to use your breadcrumbs immediately, freeze them and add them to a cooked dish straight from the freezer. Even if you don't freeze them, breadcrumbs should still be stored in an airtight container.

A final word

I hope that the above advice has been helpful and that you will now get on with making, and enjoying, your bread. Now that you have a bread machine, you'll find that making bread has never been so easy.

Notes

Please note that the yeast used in all of these recipes was easy-blend dried yeast suitable for bread-makers.

One cup = 250ml or 8 fl oz.

BREADS
&
SAVOURIES

Dark Sour Rye

In a china or plastic bowl, mix the 2 tablespoons of rye flour with the 3 tablespoons of warm milk until they form a paste. Cover the bowl and leave it in a warm place for 2 to 3 days until it smells like beer.

Transfer the rye-flour and milk mixture to the baking pan. Now add the remaining ingredients in the order in which they are listed above. Set the programme to 'DOUGH'.

Adding treacle

When the cycle has been completed, remove the dough and knead it for 2 to 3 minutes on a lightly floured surface. Shape the dough into a plump oval, cover it loosely with a damp tea towel and leave it in a warm place to prove.

Preheat the oven to 200°C/400°F /GM 6. When the dough has almost doubled in size, remove the tea towel, slash the top of the dough with a sharp knife and bake in the oven for 25 minutes. Transfer the loaf to a wire rack to cool.

Ingredients
2 tablespoons rye flour
3 tablespoons milk, warmed
1 cup milk, tepid
1 teaspoon salt
2 tablespoons black treacle
4 tablespoons butter,
  melted and cooled
2 cups rye flour
1½ cups white bread flour
½ teaspoon yeast

Dark rye

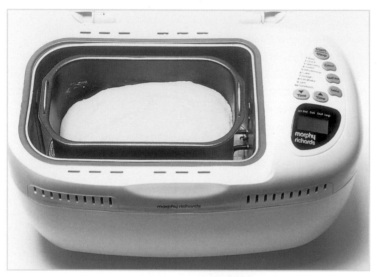

Ingredients

1 cup water, tepid

2 tablespoons black treacle

1 tablespoon honey

1 teaspoon salt

1½ cups rye flour

1½ cups white-bread flour

1 teaspoon yeast

Place all of the ingredients in the baking pan in the order in which they are listed above. Set the programme to 'BASIC'.

Adding rye flour

When the cycle has been completed, turn the loaf out onto a wire rack to cool.

Rye flour generally needs to be mixed with strong flour to lighten its texture, as it is not so rich in gluten.

The finished loaf will be dark with a close crumb. This is a good bread to serve with cold meats, pickles and cheeses.

Calzone

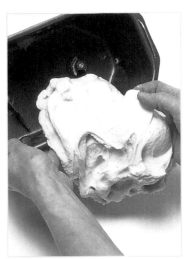
Removing proved dough

Place the first five ingredients in the baking pan in the order in which they are listed above. Set the programme to 'DOUGH'.

Place the tomato purée and chopped tomatoes in a saucepan and cook them over a gentle heat, stirring from time to time, until the mixture has thickened. Set it to one side to cool.

Preheat the oven to 200°F/400°F /GM 6. When the cycle has been completed, turn out the dough onto a lightly floured surface and knead it for 2 to 3 minutes. Divide the dough into 8 equal-sized pieces. Working with one piece at a time, roll the dough into circles measuring approximately 20.5cm (8in) across.

Mix the thickened, cooled tomatoes with the capers, mozzarella and olives. Divide this mixture between the dough rounds, ensuring that you do not place the filling beyond 1.3cm ($^1/_2$in) of the edge of the dough.

Brush the edges of the dough with a little of the beaten egg. Fold over the dough so that the filling is enclosed and pinch the edges of the dough to seal in the filling. Loosely cover each piece of dough with oiled clingfilm and leave them to prove for 30 minutes.

Preheat the oven to 200°F/400°F /GM 6. Remove the clingfilm and bake the pieces of dough in the oven for 20 to 25 minutes or until they have risen and turned golden.

Serve hot or cold.

Ingredients
1 cup water, tepid
1 teaspoon salt
2 tablespoons olive oil
3 cups white-bread flour
1 teaspoon yeast

To finish
3 tablespoons sun-dried-
  tomato purée
1 x 200g (7oz) tin chopped
  tomatoes
2 tablespoons capers
200g (7oz) mozzarella,
  cubed
100g (3$^1/_2$oz) green olives,
  pitted and roughly
  chopped
a little beaten egg

Pizza

Place the first five ingredients in the baking pan in the order in which they are listed above. Set the programme to 'DOUGH'.

Place the tomato purée and chopped tomatoes in a saucepan

approximately 35.5cm (14in) across.

Transfer the pieces of rolled dough to baking sheets, dusted with cornflour. Dividing it between the four, spread the thickened tomato mixture over the pizzas and then

Ingredients
1 cup water, tepid
1 teaspoon salt
3 tablespoons olive oil
3 cups white-bread flour
1 teaspoon yeast

To finish
2 tablespoons tomato purée
1 x 400g (14oz) tin
    chopped tomatoes
a large handful fresh basil
    leaves, torn
400g (14oz) mozzarella,
    thinly sliced
2 tablespoons fine cornmeal

Rolling pizza dough

and cook them over a gentle heat, stirring from time to time, until the mixture has thickened. Set to one side to cool.

Preheat the oven by switching it to its highest setting. When the cycle has been completed, turn out the dough onto a lightly floured surface and knead it for 2 to 3 minutes. Divide the dough into 4 equal-sized pieces. Working with one piece at a time, roll the dough into circles measuring

arrange the basil leaves and mozzarella over the top.

Bake each pizza in the top of the oven for 8 to 10 minutes. (You will need to do this in batches, so keep the uncooked pizzas at room temperature while the others are cooking.)

Multi-grain

Adding barley flour

Ingredients

1¼ cups water, tepid

4 tablespoons Greek yoghurt

2 tablespoons honey

1 teaspoon salt

2 tablespoons sunflower oil

½ cup barley flour

½ cup rye flour

1 cup granary-bread flour

¼ cup wheatgerm

¼ cup oatbran

¼ cup wholemeal-bread flour

1 cup white-bread flour

2 teaspoons yeast

Place all of the ingredients in the baking pan in the order in which they are listed above. Set the programme to 'DOUGH'.

When the cycle has been completed, turn out the dough onto a lightly floured surface and knead it for 2 to 3 minutes. Then shape the dough into a ball, place it on a lightly oiled baking tray, loosely cover it with oiled clingfilm and leave it to prove.

Preheat the oven to 200°C/400°F /GM 6. When the dough has almost doubled in size, remove the clingfilm, dust it with flour and bake it in the oven for 25 minutes or until it has turned golden and crisp. Transfer the loaf to a wire rack and leave it to cool.

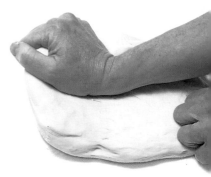

Shaping the dough

Pesto and pine nuts

Adding pesto

Ingredients
1 cup water, tepid
1 teaspoon salt
1 teaspoon honey
2 tablespoons olive oil
3¼ cups white-bread flour
1 teaspoon yeast

To finish
4 tablespoons fresh pesto
2 tablespoons pine nuts

Place the first six ingredients in the baking pan in the order in which they are listed above. Set the programme to 'DOUGH'.

When the cycle indicates, add the pesto.

When the cycle has been completed, transfer the dough to a lightly floured surface and knead it for 2 to 3 minutes Then divide the dough in half and shape each half into an oval. Transfer the ovals to a lightly oiled and floured baking tray, allowing enough room between them for them to rise. Press the pine nuts into the top of the ovals, loosely cover them with a sheet of oiled clingfilm and leave them in a warm place to prove.

Preheat the oven to 200°C/400°F/GM 6. When the dough has almost doubled in size, remove the clingfilm and bake the loaves in the oven for 20 to 25 minutes or until they are golden. Transfer the loaves to a wire rack and leave them to cool.

French country loaf

Stirring the mixture

Place 1 cup of water with 1 cup of brown-bread flour in the baking pan. Set the programme to 'DOUGH'.

At the end of the cycle, pour the mixture into a large glass or plastic bowl, loosely cover it with a damp tea towel and leave it in a warm place for 24 to 48 hours, stirring the mixture and redampening the tea towel from time to time. When the mixture smells slightly sour and its surface is a little bubbly, your sourdough starter is ready to use.

Place the sourdough starter, followed by all of the remaining ingredients in the order in which they are listed above, in the baking pan. Set the programme to 'DOUGH'.

When the cycle has been completed, transfer the dough to a lightly floured surface and knead it for 2 to 3 minutes. Shape the dough into a ball and place it on a greased baking tray. Loosely cover the dough with a sheet of oiled clingfilm and leave it in a warm place to prove.

Preheat the oven to 200°C/400°F /GM 6. When the dough has almost doubled in size, remove the clingfilm. Now sprinkle a little flour over the surface of the bread. (If you have a water spray, spray the inside of the oven with water a couple of times just before you put the loaf into bake. Although this is not essential, it will give the loaf a crisper crust.) Bake the dough in the oven for 25 minutes, then transfer the loaf to a wire rack and leave it to cool.

Ingredients

1 cup water, tepid
1 cup brown-bread flour
1 cup water, tepid
1 teaspoon salt
2 tablespoons olive oil
1 ¾ cups brown-bread flour
2 cups white-bread flour
1 teaspoon yeast

Quick courgette, garlic and ginger

Adding courgette

Ingredients

8 tablespoons (110g/4oz)
   butter, melted and cooled
1 clove garlic, crushed
1 tablespoon fresh root
   ginger, finely grated
1 cup courgette, coarsely
   grated
4 eggs
$2^{1}/_{2}$ cups plain flour
1 tablespoon baking
   powder
$^{1}/_{2}$ teaspoon bicarbonate of
   soda (baking soda)
1 teaspoon salt

In a mixing bowl, beat together the butter, garlic, ginger, courgette and eggs, then pour the mixture into the baking pan.

Sift together the flour, baking powder, bicarbonate of soda (baking soda) and salt, then add the mixture to the baking pan. Set the programme to 'CAKE'.

Halfway through the mixing cycle, check that all of the ingredients have been incorporated (if necessary, use a rubber spatula to mix in any flour that has been caught at the sides).

Once the cycle has been completed, turn out the loaf onto a wire rack and leave it to cool.

Pissaladiere

Adding anchovies

Ingredients

1 cup water, tepid
1 teaspoon salt
3 tablespoons olive oil
1 tablespoon honey
$3\frac{1}{2}$ cups white-bread flour
1 teaspoon yeast

To finish

3oz (75g) butter
4 large onions, peeled and
    thinly sliced
14 anchovy fillets canned in
    olive oil, drained and
    halved lengthways
50g (2oz) black olives, sliced
1 tablespoon olive oil

Place the first six ingredients in the baking pan in the order in which they are listed above. Set the programme to 'DOUGH'.

In a large frying pan, melt the butter and then gently cook the onions, stirring from time to time until they become golden and start to caramelise. Leave to cool.

When the cycle has been completed, transfer the dough to a lightly floured surface and knead it for 2 to 3 minutes.

Adding olives to pissaladiere

Now press the dough into the base of a lightly oiled flan tin measuring about 28cm (11in) in diameter.

Spread the cooled onion mixture evenly over the dough. Now lay the halved anchovy fillets over the onions in a crisscross pattern. Place a piece of olive in the centre of each anchovy 'diamond'. Leave at room temperature for 30 minutes.

Preheat the oven to 200°C/400°F /GM 6. Drizzle the olive oil over the flan and then bake it in the oven for 25 to 30 minutes.

This flan is best served either hot or warm.

If you don't have an eleven-inch flan tin you can make a more rustic looking pissaladiere just by shaping the dough into a rough eleven-inch circle on a lightly oiled baking sheet, covering it with the topping, and then following the recipe as above.

Provençale

Adding lardons

Ingredients

1 cup tepid water

2 tablespoons dried skimmed milk

1 teaspoon salt

2 tablespoons olive oil

1 tablespoon honey

3½ cups white-bread flour

1 teaspoon yeast

To finish

1 tablespoon olive oil

100g (3½oz) smoked lardons of bacon

25g (1oz) butter

2 large onions, peeled and thinly sliced

6 anchovy fillets canned in olive oil, torn into small pieces

50g (2oz) black olives, pitted and roughly chopped

50g (2oz) Cheddar cheese, grated

6 cherry tomatoes, cut into thin wedges

Place the first seven ingredients in the baking pan in the order in which they are listed above. Set the programme to 'DOUGH'.

Heat the olive oil in a large frying pan, then cook the lardons until they are golden and starting to crisp in places. Remove the lardons with a slotted spoon and set them to one side to cool.

Add the butter and onions to the frying pan and cook over a gentle heat until the onions have softened and are starting to turn golden. Using a slotted spoon, remove the onions and set them to one side to cool.

When the cycle has been completed, transfer the dough to a lightly floured surface and knead it for 2 to

49

3 minutes. Press the dough into a lightly oiled, shallow baking tin measuring 23 x 33cm (9 x 13in).

In a mixing bowl, combine the lardons, onions, anchovies, black olives, cheese and cherry tomatoes, then sprinkle this mixture evenly over the surface of the dough. Leave the dough to prove at room temperature for 30 minutes.

Preheat the oven to 200°C/400°F /GM 6. Bake the dough in the oven for 20 to 25 minutes, or until it is golden and crisp at the edges.

This bread makes perfect picnic fare.

Blue cheese and apple

Adding grated apple

Place the first seven ingredients in the baking pan in the order in which they are listed above. Set the programme to 'BASIC'.

When the cycle indicates, add the blue cheese.

Once the cycle has been completed, turn out the loaf onto a wire rack and leave it to cool.

Ingredients

1 cup dry cider

1 teaspoon salt

1 tablespoon honey

1 eating apple, coarsely grated

1 cup granary-bread flour

1 cup wholemeal-bread flour

1 cup white-bread flour

To finish

75g (3oz) strong blue cheese, crumbled

Quick cheese and chilli

Adding cheese

Once the cycle has been completed, turn out the loaf onto a wire rack and leave it to cool.

Ingredients

8 tablespoons (110g/4oz) butter, melted and cooled

1 large chilli, finely chopped

1 cup mature Cheddar cheese, coarsely grated

3 eggs

½ cup milk

3 cups plain flour

4 teaspoons baking powder

1 teaspoon bicarbonate of soda (baking soda)

½ teaspoon salt

In a mixing bowl, beat together the butter, chilli, cheese, eggs and milk, then pour the mixture into the baking pan.

Sift together the flour, baking powder, bicarbonate of soda (baking soda) and salt, then add the mixture to the baking pan. Set the programme to 'CAKE'.

Halfway through the mixing cycle, check that all of the ingredients have been incorporated (if necessary, use a rubber spatula to mix in any flour that has been caught at the sides).

Sieving flour

Tomato and poppy seed

Adding passata

In a mixing bowl, beat together the sunflower oil, passata and eggs, then pour the mixture into the baking pan.

Into a mixing bowl, sift together the flour, baking powder, bicarbonate of soda (baking soda) and salt, then add the poppy seeds and caster sugar. Stir well to mix the ingredients together and then add the mixture to the baking pan. Set the programme to 'CAKE'.

Halfway through the mixing cycle, check that all of the ingredients have been incorporated (if necessary, use a rubber spatula to mix in any flour that has been caught at the sides).

Once the cycle has been completed, turn out the loaf onto a wire rack and leave it to cool.

Ingredients
1/4 cup sunflower oil
1 cup ready-made passata
3 eggs
2 1/2 cups plain flour
1 tablespoon baking powder
1/2 teaspoon bicarbonate of soda (baking soda)
1/2 teaspoon salt
1/4 cup poppy seeds
1 tablespoon caster sugar

Quick Cajun carrot

Adding carrot

Ingredients

8 tablespoons (110g/4oz)
  butter, melted and cooled

¼ cup tepid milk

4 eggs

1 cup carrot, grated

2 spring onions, finely
  chopped

2½ cups plain flour

1 tablespoon baking
  powder

½ teaspoon bicarbonate of
  soda (baking soda)

1 tablespoon Cajun spice

In a mixing bowl, beat together the butter, milk, eggs, carrot and spring onions and then pour the mixture into the baking pan.

In a mixing bowl, sift together the flour, baking powder, bicarbonate of soda (baking soda) and Cajun spice and then add the mixture to the baking pan. Set the programme to 'CAKE'.

Halfway through the mixing cycle, check that all of the ingredients have been incorporated (if necessary, use a rubber spatula to mix in any flour that has been caught at the sides).

Once the cycle has been completed, turn out the loaf onto a wire rack and leave it to cool.

Oregano and tomato

Adding oregano

When the cycle has been completed, transfer the loaf to a wire rack and leave it to cool.

This bread is delicious toasted. For a quick lunch, toast a few slices, sprinkle over some grated cheese and a few slices of chopped salami, then flash back under the grill to melt the cheese.

Serve with a side salad.

Ingredients
1 cup water, tepid
$\frac{1}{2}$ cup sun-dried tomatoes, finely chopped
2 tablespoons of the oil in which the sun-dried tomatoes were preserved
1 tablespoon dried oregano
1 teaspoon salt
3 cups white-bread flour
1 teaspoon dried yeast

Place the ingredients in the baking pan in the order in which they are listed above. Set the programme to 'BASIC'.

Adding oil from sun-dried tomatoes

Potato, rosemary and Emmental

Pressing the dough

Place the first six ingredients in the baking pan in the order in which they are listed above. Set the programme to 'DOUGH'.

When the cycle has finished, transfer the dough to a floured surface and knead it for 2 to 3 minutes. Place the dough in a lightly oiled Swiss-roll tin and stretch and press it so that it covers the base. Slice the potatoes thinly and scatter the slices over the dough. Cover the dough with a sheet of oiled clingfilm and leave it to prove for 45 minutes.

Preheat the oven to 200°C/400°F /GM 6. Remove the clingfilm and drizzle a little olive oil over the dough. Bake the dough in the oven for 15 minutes. Remove the dough from the oven, sprinkle the cheese and rosemary leaves over the top and then return the dough to the oven for a further 10 minutes.

Serve the bread while it is still hot.

Ingredients
1 cup water, tepid
2 tablespoons olive oil
1 teaspoon salt
1 tablespoon fresh
  rosemary, chopped
3$\frac{1}{4}$ cups white-bread flour
1 teaspoon yeast

To finish
300g (11oz) small, waxy
  potatoes, cooked & cooled
olive oil for drizzling
75g (3oz) Emmental
  cheese, grated
Fresh rosemary leaves

Beer and mustard

Adding Dijon mustard

This bread is perfect for mopping the juices from a hearty stew or simply serving with a selection of cold meats or cheeses.

Ingredients

1 cup dark stout
$1/2$ cup tepid water
2 tablespoons sunflower oil
1 teaspoon salt
1 tablespoon black treacle
2 cups white-bread flour
$1^1/2$ cups wholemeal-bread flour
$1/2$ teaspoon yeast

To finish

3 teaspoons Dijon mustard

Place the first eight ingredients in the baking pan in the order in which they are listed above. Set the programme to 'BASIC'.

When the cycle indicates, add the mustard.

When the bread is cooked, transfer it to a wire rack and leave it to cool.

A dark, dense loaf that is given its rising power from two sources, the dried yeast and the yeast in the beer.

Treacle adds a depth of colour to the loaf, as well as adding sweetness and its distinctive flavour, which combines well with beer and mustard.

Granary

A very versatile bread good for both sweet and savoury, sandwiches, toast or simply buttered.

Adding granary flour

Ingredients
$^1/_2$ cup water, tepid
$^1/_2$ cup milk, warmed
1 teaspoon salt
3 tablespoons butter, melted and cooled
1 egg, beaten
$3^1/_2$ cups granary-bread flour
$1^1/_2$ teaspoons yeast

Place all of the ingredients in the baking pan in the order in which they are listed above. Set the programme to 'BASIC'.

When the cycle has been completed, transfer the bread to a wire rack and leave it to cool.

Granary flour has a distinctive nutty flavour which makes it one of the more popular brown breads.

Cottage loaf

Place the ingredients in the baking pan. Set the programme to 'DOUGH'.

When the cycle has been completed, transfer the dough to a floured surface and knead it for 2 to 3 minutes. Break off a quarter of the dough and put it to one side. Shape the remaining piece of dough into a ball, making sure that any folds that you may have created are in the base. Place the dough base down on a greased baking tray. Repeat the process with the smaller piece of dough, placing it well apart from the larger piece of dough on the baking sheet. Loosely cover the dough with a sheet of oiled clingfilm and leave it in a warm place to prove for 20 minutes.

Gently lift the smaller piece of dough and place it on top of the

Giving the cottage loaf its distinctive shape

larger piece. Using a well-floured finger, press down through the centre of the top piece of dough and into the bottom piece of dough. Loosely cover the dough with a sheet of oiled clingfilm and leave it to prove for a further 20 minutes.

Preheat the oven to 220°C/425°F /GM 7. Remove the clingfilm and bake the loaf in the oven for 25 minutes, or until it is golden and crisp. Transfer it to a wire rack and serve.

Ingredients
1 cup tepid water
1½ teaspoons salt
3¼ cups white-bread flour
1½ teaspoons yeast

First proving of the dough

Spiced cheese granary

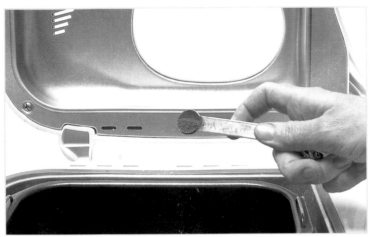

Adding cayenne pepper

Ingredients
1 cup water, tepid
1 tablespoon olive oil
1 egg, beaten
1 teaspoon salt
$\frac{1}{2}$ teaspoon caster sugar
$3\frac{1}{2}$ cups granary-bread
  flour
1 teaspoon yeast

To finish
$\frac{1}{2}$ teaspoon cayenne pepper
150g (5oz) grated mature
  Cheddar cheese

Place the first seven ingredients in the baking pan in the order in which they are listed above. Set the programme to 'BASIC'.

When the cycle indicates, add the cayenne pepper and cheese.

When the cycle has been completed, transfer the bread to a wire rack and leave it to cool for 20 minutes.

This bread is ideal as a snack and is best served warm.

Carrot and thyme

Adding carrot

spoon the carrot mixture into the centre. Fold the dough over the carrot mixture and knead it until the carrot mixture has been incorporated. Shape the dough into an oval and place it on an oiled baking sheet. Loosely cover the dough with a piece of oiled clingfilm and leave it to prove for 45 minutes, or until it has almost doubled in size.

Preheat the oven to 200°C/400°F/GM 6. Using a sharp knife, slash the top of the loaf and then bake it in the oven for 25 to 30 minutes, or until it is golden. Transfer the loaf to a wire rack and leave it to cool for 20 minutes before serving it.

Place the first six ingredients in the baking pan. Set the programme to 'DOUGH'.

Melt the butter in a small frying pan and then gently cook the onion until it is transparent. Now add the carrots and continue to cook, stirring all the while, until the carrots have been heated through and are tender. Stir in the thyme leaves and season to taste. Remove the frying pan from the heat and leave the carrot mixture to cool.

When the cycle has been completed, transfer the dough to a well-floured surface. Using your hands, flatten out the dough, then

Ingredients
$1\frac{1}{4}$ cups water, tepid
2 tablespoons olive oil
1 teaspoon honey
1 teaspoon salt
$3\frac{1}{4}$ cups white-bread flour
$1\frac{1}{2}$ teaspoons yeast

To finish
25g (1oz) butter
1 small onion, finely
    chopped
2 medium-sized carrots,
    peeled and coarsely grated
2 tablespoons fresh thyme
    leaves
salt and black pepper

Sesame seed

Scoring top of loaf

Ingredients

1 cup water, tepid
2 tablespoons sesame oil
1 teaspoon caster sugar
1 teaspoon salt
$3\frac{1}{4}$ cups white-bread flour
$1\frac{1}{2}$ teaspoons yeast

To finish

a mix of 1 small egg and 1
   tablespoon water, beaten
   together
3 tablespoons sesame seeds

Place the first six ingredients in the baking pan in the order in which they are listed above. Set the programme to 'DOUGH'.

When the cycle has finished, transfer the dough to a floured surface and shape it into a round. Place the dough on a lightly oiled baking sheet and cover it with a piece of oiled clingfilm. Leave the dough to prove until it has almost doubled in size.

Preheat the oven to 200°C/400°F /GM 6. Using the point of a sharp knife, cut a circle approximately 5mm ($\frac{1}{4}$in) deep into the centre of the loaf. Brush the dough with the egg-and-water mixture and then sprinkle the sesame seeds over the top.

Bake the loaf in the oven for 25 minutes, or until it has turned golden brown. Transfer the loaf to a wire rack and leave it to cool a little before serving it.

Sunflower seed and malt

Adding sunflower seeds

Ingredients
1 cup water, tepid
1 teaspoon salt
2 tablespoons butter, melted and cooled
1 tablespoon honey
1 tablespoon malt extract
$\frac{1}{2}$ cup sunflower seeds, coarsely chopped
2 cups wholemeal-bread flour
1 cup white-bread flour
1 teaspoon yeast

Place all of the ingredients in the baking pan in the order in which they are listed above. Set the programme to 'BASIC'.

When the cycle has been completed, transfer the loaf to a wire rack and leave it to cool.

Malt extract is generally available from Health Food shops. It has a full-bodied sweet flavour.

Sunflower seeds are a tasty addition to this bread and, because they are rich in iron, they are also nutritionally beneficial.

Olive

Adding mixed olives

example, try olives with chillies, or garlic, or a stuffed olive of your choice.

A delicious bread to serve with an Italian meal or simply a tomato salad and cheese.

Ingredients

1 cup water, tepid
2 tablespoons olive oil
$\frac{1}{2}$ teaspoon salt
3 cups white-bread flour
$1\frac{1}{2}$ teaspoons yeast

To finish

1 cup mixed olives, pitted

Place the first five ingredients in the baking pan in the order in which they are listed above. Set the programme to 'BASIC'.

When the cycle indicates, add the olives.

When the cycle has been completed, transfer the bread to a wire rack and leave it to cool.

There are a wide variety of olives available now in most major supermarkets. You could vary the flavour of this bread by using different varieties of olives. For

Mustard

Adding wholegrain mustard

Place the first eight ingredients in the baking pan in the order in which they are listed above. Set the programme to 'DOUGH'.

When the cycle has been completed, transfer the dough to a lightly floured surface, knead and shape it into a round. Place the dough on a well-greased baking tray, cover it with a piece of lightly oiled clingfilm and leave it to prove in a warm place.

Preheat the oven to 200°C/400°F /GM 6. When the dough has almost doubled in size, remove the clingfilm, brush the loaf with the beaten egg and sprinkle over the black mustard seeds. Using a pair of kitchen scissors, snip into the surface of the loaf.Bake the loaf in the oven for 25 minutes, or until it is golden and crisp. Transfer the loaf to a wire rack and leave it to cool for 15 minutes before serving it.

Ingredients
1 cup water, tepid
2 tablespoons butter, melted
3 teaspoons powdered English mustard
2 tablespoons wholegrain mustard
$1/2$ teaspoon turmeric
$1/2$ teaspoon salt
3 cups white-bread flour
1 teaspoon yeast

To finish
1 egg, beaten
1 tablespoon black mustard seeds

Cheese and herb

Adding cheese

Place the first five ingredients in the baking pan in the order in which they are listed above. Set the programme to 'QUICK'.

When the cycle indicates, add the chives, parsley, basil, Parmesan, black pepper and Cheddar.

When the cycle has finished, transfer the bread to a wire rack and leave it to cool for 20 minutes.

Ideal as a snack, this bread is best served warm.

As you gain more confidence with your bread machine you may like to try using different combinations of herbs in place of the ones suggested, fresh thyme, rosemary, coriander, the choice is yours.

Ingredients
$3/4$ cup water, tepid
1 tablespoon basil-flavoured olive oil
1 teaspoon salt
2 cups white-bread flour
1 teaspoon yeast

To finish
2 tablespoons fresh chives, chopped
2 tablespoons fresh flat-leaf parsley, chopped
2 tablespoons fresh basil, chopped
$1/2$ cup Parmesan cheese, grated
$1/2$ teaspoon black pepper, freshly ground
1 cup mature Cheddar cheese, grated

Roasted peppers and red onion

Adding peppers

Ingredients
1 cup water, tepid
1 tablespoon olive oil
1 teaspoon salt
3¼ cups white flour
1 teaspoon yeast

To finish
1 red onion
2 yellow peppers
  (capsicums)
1 red pepper (capsicums)
2 tablespoons olive oil

Place the first five ingredients in the baking pan in the order in which they are listed above. Set the programme to 'DOUGH'. Preheat the oven to 200°C/400°F/GM 6.

Peel the onion and de-seed the peppers. Cut the onion into thin wedges, working from top to bottom, and chop the peppers into bite-sized chunks. In a mixing bowl, toss together the peppers and onions in the olive oil, then transfer them to a roasting tray. Roast the vegetables in the oven for 25 minutes, or until they have cooked through and are tender. Remove the vegetables from the oven and set them aside to cool.

When the cycle has been completed, transfer the dough to a lightly floured surface and knead it briefly. Using a floured rolling pin, roll out the dough and then stretch it into an oblong measuring approximately 30.5 x 23cm (12 x 9in). Sprinkle the cooled roasted-pepper-and-onion mixture over the dough, leaving a gap of 1.3cm ($\frac{1}{2}$in) all round. Taking the long edge nearest to you, roll up the dough as you would a Swiss roll, thereby encasing the vegetables. Pinch the edges together to seal them. Carefully transfer the dough to a lightly greased and floured baking sheet and cover it with a sheet of oiled clingfilm. Leave the dough to prove in a warm place for approximately 45 minutes.

Preheat the oven to 220°C/425°F/GM 7. When the dough has almost doubled in size, remove the clingfilm and bake the loaf in the oven for 10 minutes. Reduce the heat to 190°C/375°F/GM 5

and bake the loaf for a further 15 to 20 minutes, or until the bread is golden. Carefully transfer the loaf to a wire rack and leave it to cool.

This bread is best served slightly warm.

Cheese and tomato

Adding tomato ketchup

Ingredients
1 cup water, tepid
1 tablespoon olive oil
1 medium-sized egg, beaten
3 tablespoons tomato
  ketchup
1 teaspoon salt
1 teaspoon black pepper,
  freshly ground
3½ cups white-bread flour
1 teaspoon yeast

To finish
2 cups Cheddar cheese,
  grated

Place the first eight ingredients in the baking pan in the order in which they are listed above. Set the programme to 'BASIC'.

When the cycle indicates, add the cheese.

When the cycle has been completed, transfer the loaf to a wire rack and leave it to cool.

This bread is delicious, so don't be put off by the inclusion of tomato ketchup. Enjoy it toasted, served with soup or as part of a packed lunch.

To make a tasty breakfast, beat one egg with a little milk and season with salt and pepper. Dip slices of the bread into this seasoned egg mixture, then fry in a non-stick

frying pan until both sides of the bread are golden.

Serve this with bacon or baked beans for a breakfast that will keep you going until lunch.

If you want to pep it up a little more, add a dash of Worcestershire sauce to the beaten egg before adding the bread.

Pittas

Shaping pitta bread

and leave them to rise for a further 15 minutes. Preheat the oven to its highest setting.

When the dough has risen, bake the pittas in the oven for 5 minutes. (If they need a little longer, reduce the oven temperature to 190°C/ 375°F/GM 5 and bake them for a further 2 to 3 minutes.) Transfer the pittas to a wire rack and cover them with a clean tea towel. Leave the pittas to cool a little before serving them.

Ingredients
³/₄ cup water, tepid
1 tablespoon sunflower oil
1 teaspoon salt
3 cups white-bread flour
1 teaspoon yeast

Place all of the ingredients in the baking pan in the order in which they are listed above. Set the programme to 'DOUGH'.

When the cycle has been completed, transfer the dough to a floured surface and knead it for 2 minutes. Divide the dough into 10 equal-sized pieces and shape each into a ball. Place the balls on a lightly greased and floured baking tray, cover them with a sheet of oiled clingfilm and leave them to rise for 20 minutes.

Using a floured rolling pin, roll each ball into an oval shape approximately 5mm (¹/₄in) thick. Return the pittas to the baking tray

Blue cheese and sage

Scoring top of loaf

Ingredients
1 cup water, tepid
1 tablespoon olive oil
1 teaspoon salt
2½ cups white-bread flour
1 cup fine cornmeal
1 teaspoon yeast

To finish
1 medium-sized egg, beaten
100g (3½oz) blue cheese
12 fresh sage leaves

Place the first six ingredients in the baking pan in the order in which they are listed above. Set the programme to 'DOUGH'.

When the cycle has been completed, transfer the dough to a lightly floured surface and knead it for 2 to 3 minutes. Using a lightly floured rolling pin, roll out the dough into an oblong measuring approximately 40.5 x 23cm (16 x 9in). Brush the dough with some of the beaten egg, then crumble the cheese evenly over the top. Lay the sage leaves down the length of one half of the dough. Taking one long edge, fold the dough in half to enclose the cheese and sage. Pinch the edges to seal them, pressing down gently on the dough to release any air pockets as you do so. Transfer the dough to a greased baking tray and cover it with a piece of oiled clingfilm. Leave the dough to prove for about 45 minutes. (Although it will increase in size, it won't double due to the amount of cornmeal that it contains.)

Preheat the oven to 200°C/400°F /GM 6. Brush the top of the dough with the rest of the beaten egg. Using a sharp, dampened knife, make a series of diagonal cuts on top of the loaf to create a diamond pattern. Bake the loaf in the oven for 25 minutes, or until it is golden. Transfer the loaf to a wire rack and leave it to cool for 10 minutes.

This bread is delicious when served warm with soup or salad.

Camembert and red onion

Adding onion

Place the first seven ingredients in the baking pan. Set the programme to 'DOUGH'.

In a small frying pan, sauté the onion pieces in the butter and olive oil until they have softened and become transparent. Remove the pan from the heat and allow the onions to cool.

When the cycle has finished, transfer the dough to a floured surface and knead it for 2 minutes. Using a floured rolling pin, roll out the dough into a circle that it is big enough to enclose the cheese completely. Place the cheese in the centre of the dough and top it with the cooled onions. Brush the edges of the dough with some of the beaten egg and then bring up them

up so that the cheese and onions are enclosed. Pinch the edges to seal them. Place the dough on a baking sheet that has been lightly oiled and dusted with flour. Loosely cover the dough with a sheet of oiled clingfilm and leave it to prove in a warm place.

Preheat the oven to 200°C/400°F /GM 6. When the dough has puffed up, brush it with the rest of the beaten egg and then bake it in the oven for 25 minutes, or until it is golden and crisp. Leave it to cool for 15 minutes.

To enjoy it at its best, this bread must be eaten warm.

Ingredients

1 cup water, tepid
1 tablespoon olive oil
1 teaspoon salt
2 tablespoons honey
$\frac{1}{2}$ teaspoon mustard powder
$3\frac{1}{4}$ cups white-bread flour
1 teaspoon yeast

To finish

1 large red onion, finely chopped
1 tablespoon butter
1 tablespoon olive oil
1 whole Camembert cheese, weighing approximately 250g (9oz) or 10cm (4in) in diameter
1 egg, beaten

Walnut

Adding flour

Ingredients
1 cup water, tepid
2 tablespoons walnut oil
1 teaspoon salt
1 teaspoon caster sugar
3 cups white-bread flour
1 teaspoon yeast

To finish
100g ($3\frac{1}{2}$oz) walnuts,
  roughly chopped

Place the first six ingredients in the baking pan. Set the programme to 'BASIC'.

When the cycle indicates, add the walnuts.

At the end of the programme, transfer the bread to a wire rack and leave it to cool.

This bread tastes particularly good when served with cheese and fruit. It also makes a great accompaniment for salads.

Walnut oil is available from major supermarkets and good food stores. It is important to store it in a cool, dark place and it will keep for up to three months once opened. It makes a very tasty addition to salad dressings or sauces. In France it goes by the name of *huile de noix*.

Olive and oregano

Adding black olives

Adding yeast

Ingredients
1 cup water, tepid
2 tablespoons olive oil
1 teaspoon salt
3 cups white-bread flour
1 teaspoon yeast

To finish
2 teaspoons dried oregano
50g (2oz) black olives,
   pitted and chopped

Place the first five ingredients in the baking pan. Set the programme to 'BASIC'.

When the cycle indicates, add the oregano and olives.

At the end of the cycle, transfer the bread to a wire rack and leave it to cool.

This tasty savoury bread is a perfect addition to any Italian meal. You can use green olives if you prefer.

For a quick and easy canape, toast thin slices of the bread, then cut into bite-size pieces. Top each piece with a little soft creamy cheese and serve with drinks.

Corn and chilli

Adding cornmeal

Ingredients
$^2/_3$ cup water, tepid
1 tablespoon butter, melted and cooled
1 tablespoon honey
1 teaspoon chilli flakes
$^1/_2$ teaspoon salt
2 tablespoons fromage frais
$1^1/_2$ cups white-bread flour
$^1/_2$ cup fine cornmeal
$1^1/_2$ teaspoons yeast

Place the ingredients in the baking pan in the order in which they are listed above. Set the programme to 'BASIC'.

When the cycle has been completed, transfer the loaf to a wire rack and leave it to cool for 20 minutes before serving.

This bread is ideally suited to serving with a hearty soup or stew. Once having made it you can decide whether you like it a bit more or less spicy. This can be easily achieved by adjusting the amount of chilli flakes.

Cornmeal is available in three different grades – fine, medium and coarse. It is made from dried corn kernels.

Spiced sweet potato

Place the first six ingredients in the baking pan in the order in which they are listed above. Set the programme to 'DOUGH'.

In a small frying pan, sauté the chopped onion in the olive oil until the onion pieces have softened and become transparent. Add the pimento and cayenne pepper and continue to cook for 1 minute. Remove the pan from the heat and then stir in the mashed sweet potato.

When the cycle has been completed, transfer the dough to a floured surface and knead in the mashed-potato mixture (the mixture will be quite wet, but work quickly, adding a bit more flour if necessary). Place the dough in a lightly oiled baking tin measuring approximately 33 x 23cm (13 x 9in), pressing it out so that it covers the base of the tin evenly. Cover the dough with a piece of oiled clingfilm and leave it to prove until it has almost doubled in size.

Preheat the oven to 200°C/400°F /GM 6. Remove the clingfilm and bake the dough in the oven for 20 to 25 minutes, or until it is golden and has cooked through. Transfer the loaf to a wire rack and leave it to cool.

Ingredients

1 cup water, tepid
1 tablespoon olive oil
1 teaspoon salt
1 teaspoon honey
$3\frac{1}{2}$ cups white-bread flour
1 teaspoon yeast

To finish

1 small onion, finely
  chopped
1 tablespoon olive oil
1 teaspoon pimento
$\frac{1}{4}$ teaspoon cayenne pepper
250g (9oz) sweet potato,
  cooked, cooled and
  mashed

Folding spiced sweet potato into dough

Naans

Adding yoghurt

lightly floured rolling pin, roll and shape each piece into a teardrop shape measuring approximately 5mm ($\frac{1}{4}$in) thick. Place the naans on a lightly oiled and floured baking sheet and cover them with a damp tea towel. Leave them to prove for 20 minutes.

Heat the grill to its highest setting. Remove the tea towel and grill each naan for 2 to 3 minutes, or until small, golden spots start to appear on the surface, then turn it over and repeat the process on the other side.

Either serve the naans at once or reheat them by wrapping them in aluminium foil and placing them in a hot oven for 5 minutes.

Place the ingredients in the baking pan in the order in which they are listed above. Set the programme to 'DOUGH'.

When the cycle has finished, transfer the dough to a floured surface and knead it for 2 to 3 minutes. Divide the dough into 8 equal-sized pieces, then, using a

Ingredients
$\frac{3}{4}$ cup water, tepid
2 tablespoons sunflower oil
1 teaspoon honey
4 tablespoons plain yoghurt
1 teaspoon salt
3 cups white-bread flour
1 teaspoon yeast

Shaping naan bread

Focaccia

Ingredients

1 cup water, tepid
1 teaspoon yeast
4 tablespoons olive oil
3 cups white-bread flour
1 teaspoon salt

To finish

2 tablespoons olive oil
1 tablespoon sea salt
1 tablespoon fresh rosemary
   leaves

Pour the tepid water into a large mixing bowl, add the yeast, olive oil and 1 cup of the white-bread flour and mix together well. Cover the bowl with a sheet of clingfilm and leave it in a warm place for 2 to 3 hours.

Pour the yeast mixture into the baking pan and then add the remaining white-bread flour and salt. Set the programme to 'DOUGH'.

When the cycle has finished, transfer the dough to a floured surface and knead it briefly. Place the dough in a shallow baking tray measuring 23 x 33cm (9 x 13in) and press it out so that it covers the base. Cover the dough with a sheet of oiled clingfilm and leave it to prove until it has almost doubled in size.

Preheat the oven to 220°C/425°F /GM 7. Brush your fingertips with some of the olive oil and randomly dimple the surface of the dough by pushing into it. Drizzle the remaining olive oil over the dough and then sprinkle over the sea salt and rosemary leaves. Bake the dough in the oven for 25 minutes. When it has cooked through, transfer the focaccia to a wire rack and leave it to cool.

Dimpling focaccia

Potato, onion and thyme

Adding fresh herbs

Place the first six ingredients in the baking pan in the order in which they are listed above. Set the programme to 'DOUGH'.

In a frying pan, sauté the onion pieces in the olive oil until they have softened and become transparent. Now stir in the thyme leaves and sauté for a further 1 to 2 minutes. Remove the pan from the heat and stir in the mashed potatoes, mixing the ingredients together well. Season to taste.

When the cycle indicates, add the potato mixture.

When the cycle has finished, remove the dough from the baking pan and press it into a fluted tart tin measuring 28cm (11in) in diameter (if the dough is quite wet, flour your hands well). Cover the dough with a sheet of oiled clingfilm and leave it to prove until it has almost doubled in size.

Preheat the oven to 200°C/400°F/GM 6. Remove the clingfilm and bake the dough in the oven for 20 minutes, or until a golden crust has formed.

This is a rather moist bread, making it perfect for serving warm with stews or other dishes that have tasty juices to mop up.

Kneading the bread

Ingredients
1 cup water, tepid
2 tablespoons olive oil
1 teaspoon salt
2½ cups white-bread flour
1 cup fine cornmeal
1 teaspoon yeast

To finish
1 small onion, finely chopped
1 tablespoon olive oil
2 tablespoons fresh thyme leaves
200g (7oz) mashed potatoes, cold
salt and freshly ground black pepper

Three cheese and sun-dried tomato

Adding olive oil

Place the first nine ingredients in the baking pan in the order in which they are listed above. Set the programme to 'DOUGH'.

At the end of the cycle, transfer the dough to a lightly floured surface. Now knead the dough for 2 to 3 minutes. Using a rolling pin, roll out the dough into a rectangle measuring approximately 35 x 20cm (13 ³/₄ x 8in). (If the dough is too springy at this stage, leave it to rest for 5 minutes before continuing.) Lay the slices of mozzarella over the dough, leaving a 2cm (³/₄in) border around the edges. Now crumble over the blue cheese. Taking one of the long edges, roll up the dough to enclose the filling and then pinch the edges to seal them. Transfer the dough to a lightly oiled baking tray, placing it seam side down. Cover the dough with a sheet of oiled clingfilm and leave it to prove in a warm place.

Preheat the oven to 200°C/400°F /GM 6. When the dough has almost doubled in size, remove the clingfilm, brush the surface with the olive oil and sprinkle over the sea salt. Bake the dough in the oven for 30 to 35 minutes or until it is golden and crisp. Transfer the loaf to a wire rack and leave it to cool for 15 minutes before cutting it into slices and serving it.

This bread tastes particularly delicious when toasted.

Ingredients
1 cup water, tepid
1 tablespoon olive oil
2 tablespoons sun-dried
  tomato paste
1 teaspoon caster sugar
1 teaspoon salt
2 tablespoons dried
  skimmed milk
3 tablespoons Parmesan
  cheese, freshly grated
3¹/₄ cups white flour
1¹/₂ teaspoons yeast

To finish
100g (3¹/₂oz) mozzarella
  cheese, thinly sliced
75g (3oz) blue cheese
1 tablespoon olive oil
1 teaspoon coarse sea salt

SWEET LOAVES

&

CAKES

Syrup oatie

Adding oat bran

Preheat the oven to 200°F/400°F /GM 6. Remove the clingfilm, brush the surface of the dough with the melted butter and then sprinkle over the rolled oats.

Bake the dough in the oven for 20 to 25 minutes or until it has turned golden and is cooked through. Transfer the bread to a wire rack to cool.

Ingredients
1 cup water, tepid
1 tablespoon dried skimmed milk
2 tablespoons golden syrup
2 tablespoons butter, melted and cooled
$\frac{1}{2}$ teaspoon salt
$1\frac{1}{2}$ cups white-bread flour
1 cup fine oatbran
1 teaspoon yeast

To finish
1 tablespoon melted butter
1 tablespoon rolled oats

Place the first eight ingredients in the baking pan in the order in which they are listed above. Set the programme to 'DOUGH'.

When the programme has been completed, turn out the dough and knead it on a lightly floured surface for 2 to 3 minutes.

Shape the dough into a ball and place it on a lightly oiled and floured baking sheet. Cover the dough loosely with a sheet of lightly oiled clingfilm and leave it to prove in a warm place until it has almost doubled in size.

Oats go on dough before baking

115

Muesli bread

Adding muesli to machine

Adding skimmed milk

Ingredients
1 cup water, tepid
2 tablespoons dried
  skimmed milk
1 tablespoon honey
$\frac{1}{2}$ teaspoon salt
2 tablespoons sunflower oil
2 cups white-bread flour
$1\frac{1}{2}$ cups muesli
1 teaspoon yeast

Place all of the ingredients in the baking pan in the order in which they are listed above. Set the programme to 'BASIC'.

At the end of the cycle, turn out the bread onto a wire rack and leave it to cool.

This bread is perfect for breakfast on the run. Either with butter and jam or toasted, it is filling and nutritious.

It would also be good served with a nice piece of cheese and fruit for an easy lunch or snack.

Chocolate nut twist

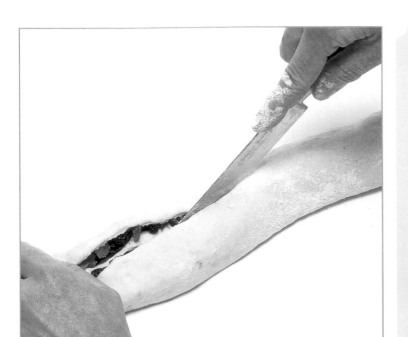

Splitting chocolate nut twist

Ingredients

$^1/_2$ cup milk, tepid
$^1/_2$ cup water, tepid
2 eggs, beaten
3 tablespoons butter,
  melted and cooled
2 tablespoons caster sugar
$^1/_2$ teaspoon salt
$3^1/_2$ cups white-bread flour
1 teaspoon yeast

To finish

75g (3oz) butter
75g (3oz) caster sugar
1 egg, beaten
100g ($3^1/_2$oz) chopped
  hazelnuts, toasted
75g (3oz) dark-chocolate
  chips

Place the first eight ingredients in the baking pan in the order in which they are listed above. Set the programme to 'DOUGH'.

In a mixing bowl, cream the butter and caster sugar together until the mixture is light and fluffy. Now beat in the beaten egg, hazelnuts and chocolate chips. Set to one side.

When the dough is ready, turn it out onto a lightly floured surface and knead it for 2 to 3 minutes. Using a lightly floured rolling pin, roll out the dough to form a rectangle about 51x 25.5cm (20 by 10in) in size. Spread the creamed chocolate and nut mixture over the top.

Taking one of the long edges, roll up the dough so that it encloses the filling, pinching the long edge as you finish to seal it shut. Using a large, sharp knife, cut the dough in half widthways to make two rolls.

119

Taking one roll at a time, and using the same sharp knife, split the first roll in half lengthways, then twist the two cut pieces together, keeping the cut surface facing upwards. Pinch the ends together to seal them. Repeat this procedure with the other roll.

Place each twist on a lightly oiled and floured baking tray, allowing room for them to rise. Loosely cover them with a sheet of oiled clingfilm and leave them to prove for 45 minutes.

Preheat the oven to 200°C/400°F /GM 6. Remove the clingfilm and bake the twists in the oven for 25 minutes, or until they are golden and cooked through.

Transfer the twists to a wire rack and leave them to cool, but not for too long because they are best eaten warm.

Chocolate coil

Coiling chocolate coil

Ingredients
1 cup milk, tepid
3 tablespoons caster sugar
1 teaspoon salt
3 tablespoons butter,
   melted and cooled
$3\frac{1}{4}$ cups white-bread flour
1 teaspoon yeast

To finish
100g ($3\frac{1}{2}$oz) good-quality
   dark chocolate, chopped
1 egg, beaten

Place the first six ingredients in the baking pan in the order in which they are listed above. Set the programme to 'DOUGH'.

When the cycle has been completed, transfer the dough to a lightly floured surface and knead it for 2 to 3 minutes. Add the chopped chocolate and knead it into the dough until it has been well incorporated. Shape the dough into a long sausage shape with tapered ends. Transfer the dough to a lightly oiled and floured baking tray and

then shape it into a coil, tucking under the end to finish. Loosely cover the dough with a sheet of oiled clingfilm and leave it in a warm place to prove for approximately 45 minutes.

Preheat the oven to 200°C/400°F /GM 6. When the dough has almost doubled in size, remove the clingfilm and brush it with the beaten egg. Bake the dough in the oven for 25 minutes, or until it is golden. Transfer the coil to a wire rack and leave it to cool.

Lemon and ginger quick bread

Adding lemon zest

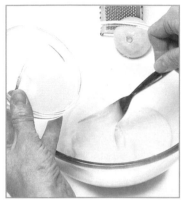

Mixing lemon juice into the mixture

Ingredients

3 eggs
$^{1}/_{3}$ cup sunflower oil
$^{1}/_{4}$ cup freshly squeezed
  lemon juice
zest of 1 lemon
$2^{1}/_{2}$ cups plain flour
2 teaspoons baking powder
$^{1}/_{2}$ teaspoon bicarbonate of
  soda (baking soda)
$1^{1}/_{2}$ teaspoons powdered
  ginger
$^{1}/_{2}$ cup soft brown sugar
$^{1}/_{2}$ cup caster sugar

In a mixing bowl, beat together the eggs, sunflower oil, lemon juice and lemon zest. Pour the ingredients into the baking pan.

Sift together the flour, baking powder, bicarbonate of soda (baking soda) and ginger, then add the brown sugar and the caster sugar. Stir the ingredients until they are well mixed, then add the mixture to the baking pan. Set the programme to 'CAKE'.

Halfway through the mixing cycle, check that all of the ingredients have been incorporated (if necessary, use a rubber spatula to mix in any flour that has been caught at the sides).

Once the cycle has been completed, turn out the loaf onto a wire rack and leave it to cool.

Quick marmalade and citrus

Adding juice

powder and bicarbonate of soda (baking soda) and then add them to the baking pan. Set the programme to 'CAKE'.

Halfway through the mixing cycle, check that all of the ingredients have been incorporated (if necessary, use a rubber spatula to mix in any flour that has been caught at the sides).

Once the cycle has been completed, turn out the loaf onto a wire rack and leave it to cool.

Ingredients
110g (4oz) butter
6 tablespoons marmalade
1 orange
1 lime
1 lemon
4 eggs
2$\frac{1}{2}$ cups plain flour
$\frac{1}{2}$ cup caster sugar
1 tablespoon baking powder
$\frac{1}{2}$ teaspoon bicarbonate of soda (baking soda)

Place the butter and marmalade in a saucepan and cook over a gentle heat, stirring from time to time until they have melted. Set to one side to cool.

Finely grate the zest from the orange, lime and lemon. In a mixing bowl, beat together the cooled butter, marmalade, zest and eggs until the ingredients are well combined. Add to this the juice from half of the orange, lime and lemon and beat again, then pour the mixture into the baking pan.

Into a mixing bowl, sift together the flour, caster sugar, baking

Quick blueberry and almond

Adding blueberries

been incorporated (if necessary, use a rubber spatula to mix in any flour that has been caught at the sides).

When the cycle indicates, add the blueberries.

Once the cycle has been completed, turn out the loaf onto a wire rack and leave it to cool.

Ingredients

8 tablespoons (110g/4oz) butter, melted and cooled
3 eggs
$\frac{1}{2}$ cup ground almonds
$\frac{1}{2}$ teaspoon almond essence
2 cups plain flour
1 tablespoon baking powder
$\frac{1}{2}$ teaspoon bicarbonate of soda (baking soda)
$\frac{2}{3}$ cup caster sugar
$\frac{1}{2}$ teaspoon salt
125g (4$\frac{1}{2}$oz) fresh blueberries

In a mixing bowl, beat together the butter, eggs, ground almonds and almond essence, then pour the mixture into the baking pan.

Into a mixing bowl, sift together the flour, baking powder, ground almonds, bicarbonate of soda (baking soda), caster sugar and salt and then add the mixture to the baking pan. Set the programme to 'CAKE'.

Halfway through the mixing cycle, check that all of the ingredients have

Quick apple

Adding apple to mixture

In a mixing bowl, beat together the butter, eggs and apple sauce, then pour the mixture into the baking pan.

Into a mixing bowl, sift together the flour, baking powder, bicarbonate of soda (baking soda), salt and cinnamon, then add the brown sugar. Stir well to mix together the ingredients and then add the mixture to the baking pan. Set the programme to 'CAKE'.

Halfway through the mixing cycle, check that all of the ingredients have been incorporated (if necessary, use a rubber spatula to mix in any flour that has been caught at the sides).

Once the cycle has been completed, turn out the loaf onto a wire rack and leave it to cool.

Ingredients
8 tablespoons (110g/4oz) butter, melted and cooled

3 eggs

1 cup apple sauce

$2\frac{1}{2}$ cups plain flour

1 tablespoon baking powder

$\frac{1}{2}$ teaspoon bicarbonate of soda (baking soda)

$\frac{1}{2}$ teaspoon salt

1 teaspoon cinnamon

$\frac{1}{2}$ cup soft brown sugar

Quick pineapple, coconut and banana

Adding beaten eggs

Ingredients
8 tablespoons (110g/4oz)
   butter, melted and cooled
1 banana, mashed
1 cup pineapple, crushed
4 eggs, beaten
2½ cups plain flour
1 tablespoon baking
   powder
½ teaspoon bicarbonate of
   soda (baking soda)
1 cup desiccated coconut
½ cup soft brown sugar

In a mixing bowl, beat together the butter, banana, pineapple and eggs, then add the mixture to the baking pan.

Into a mixing bowl, sift the flour, baking powder and bicarbonate of soda (baking soda), then stir in the desiccated coconut and brown sugar. Add the mixture to the baking pan and set the programme to 'CAKE'.

Halfway through the mixing cycle, check that all of the ingredients have been incorporated (if necessary, use a rubber spatula to mix in any flour that has been caught at the sides).

Once the cycle has been completed, turn out the loaf onto a wire rack and leave it to cool.

Stuffed-apple and mixed-fruit plait

Creating the plait

Place the first seven ingredients in the baking pan in the order in which they are listed above. Set the programme to 'DOUGH'.

When the cycle has finished, transfer the dough to a floured surface and knead it briefly. Using a lightly floured rolling pin, roll out the dough into a rectangle measuring approximately 40.5 x 25.5cm (16 x 10in). Arrange the apple slices evenly down the central third of the dough, leaving a gap of about 2.5cm (1in) at each end. Spread the dried mixed fruits over the apples. Cut the butter into small pieces, combine it with the sugar in a mixing bowl, then sprinkle the mixture evenly over the dried fruits.

Using a sharp knife, make a diagonal cut at each corner, stopping about 1.3cm (¹/₂in) from the filling.

Brush the two short ends with the beaten egg and fold them over the filling. Now make diagonal cuts down each long side of the dough, about 2.5cm (1in) apart, and brush them with beaten egg. Plait the dough over the filling, taking alternating strips of dough from each side until all of the strips have been used up. Carefully transfer the dough to a lightly greased baking tray. Loosely cover the dough with a sheet of oiled clingfilm and leave it to rest for 20 minutes.

Preheat the oven to 200°C/400°F /GM 6. Remove the clingfilm, brush the dough with beaten egg, then bake it in the oven for 20 to 25 minutes or until it is golden.

Serve hot or cold.

Ingredients
1 cup water, tepid
2 eggs, beaten
50g (2oz) butter, softened
3 tablespoons caster sugar
1 teaspoon salt
3¹/₂ cups white-bread flour
1¹/₂ teaspoons yeast

To finish
2 eating apples, peeled,
   cored and thinly sliced
110g (4oz) dried mixed
   fruits
25g (1oz) butter
1 tablespoon caster sugar
Beaten egg for glazing

Glazing

Cranberry and orange

Ingredients

1 cup freshly squeezed
  orange juice
2 tablespoons butter,
  softened
1 egg, beaten
2 tablespoons caster sugar
$\frac{1}{2}$ teaspoon salt
$3\frac{1}{2}$ cups white-bread flour
1 teaspoon yeast

To finish

juice of 1 orange
75g (3oz) dried cranberries
zest of 1 orange

Place the first seven ingredients in the baking pan in the order in which they are listed above. Set the programme to 'DOUGH'.

Place the juice of the orange and the cranberries in a bowl and set it to one side.

When the programme has been completed, remove the dough. Now strain the cranberries and orange zest, add to the dough and knead them in until they have been well incorporated. (You may need to add a little extra flour to make the process easier.) Shape the dough into a long sausage shape, roll it up into a coil and then place it on a lightly oiled and floured baking tray. Loosely cover the dough with a damp tea towel and leave it to prove until nearly doubled in size.

Preheat the oven to 200°C/400°F /GM 6. When the dough has almost doubled in size, remove the tea towel and bake it in the oven for 20 or 25 minutes, or until it is golden and has cooked through. Transfer the loaf to a wire rack and leave it to cool.

Shaping the loaf

Lardy cake

Lardy cake ingredients

Ingredients
1 cup water, tepid
2 tablespoons dried
   skimmed milk
1 tablespoon honey
1 tablespoon butter, melted
   and cooled
$\frac{1}{2}$ teaspoon salt
3 cups white-bread flour
1 teaspoon yeast

To finish
125g ($4\frac{1}{2}$oz) mixed
   sultanas and currants
50g (2oz) chopped mixed
   peel
1 teaspoon ground mixed
   spice
100g ($3\frac{1}{2}$oz) soft dark-
   brown sugar
100g ($3\frac{1}{2}$oz) lard

Place the first seven ingredients in the baking pan in the order in which they are listed above. Set the programme to 'DOUGH'.

When the cycle has been completed, transfer the dough to a lightly floured surface. Knock down the dough and, using a lightly floured rolling pin, roll it out into an oblong measuring approximately 15.25 x 45.75cm (6 x 18in). With one of the short sides nearest to you, sprinkle the bottom two-thirds of the dough with one-third of the sultanas and currants, mixed peel, mixed spice and brown sugar. Cut one-third of the lard into small pieces and add them to the mixture. Taking the top piece of dough that has not been used, fold it over half of the filling, then fold up the bottom (filled) piece of dough over this. (You should now have folded the dough into three layers, like folding a letter.) Seal the open edges with a rolling pin, then give the dough a quarter turn to the left (the completely enclosed side should always be on

Folding lardy cake

the left) and repeat the procedure twice more until all of the filling has been used up. Allow the dough to rest for 10 minutes.

Lightly grease two round cake tins 17.75cm (7in) in diameter. Roll out the dough into an oblong measuring approximately 33 x 15.25cm (13 x 6in) and then cut it in half width-ways. Pinch the cut edge to seal it.

Transfer each piece of dough to a prepared tin, tucking under the corners to make it fit. Cover both pieces of dough with a damp tea towel and leave them to prove at room temperature until they have almost doubled in size. (Do not leave them anywhere too warm, otherwise the lard will melt.)

Preheat the oven to 200°C/400°F /GM 6. Bake the dough pieces in the oven for 25 minutes, or until they until golden. Allow them to cool in their tins for 10 minutes before turning them out.

Stuffed-fruit twist

Place the first eight ingredients in the baking pan in the order in which they are listed above. Set the programme to 'DOUGH'.

In a bowl, mix together the currants, sultanas, raisins, figs and apricots and then set to one side.

In a mixing bowl, and using a wooden spoon, cream together the butter and caster sugar until the mixture is light and fluffy. Gradually add the beaten egg, mixing well between each addition. Finally, beat in the ground almonds and almond essence.

When the dough cycle has been completed, turn out the dough onto a floured surface and knead it for 2 to 3 minutes. Using a floured rolling pin, roll out the dough into a rectangle measuring approximately 56 x 25.5cm (22 x 10in). Spread the almond mixture evenly over the dough, then sprinkle over the dried-fruit mixture.

Taking one of the long edges, roll up the dough as you would a swiss roll, pinching the edge to seal it. Now take a sharp knife and cut the roll in half down its length. Carefully shape the two pieces of dough into a twist, ensuring that the cut edges remain facing upwards. Gently transfer the twist to a lightly greased

Ingredients
- $3/4$ cup water, tepid
- 2 tablespoons dried skimmed milk
- 3 tablespoons unsalted butter, melted and cooled
- 1 egg, beaten
- 3 tablespoons honey
- 1 teaspoon salt
- 3 cups white-bread flour
- 1 teaspoon yeast

Making the twist

To finish
75g (3oz) currants
75g (3oz) sultanas
50g (2oz) golden raisins
100g (3½oz) dried, ready-
   to-eat figs, roughly
   chopped
100g (3½oz) dried, ready-
   to-eat apricots, roughly
   chopped
75g (3oz) butter
50g (2oz) caster sugar
1 egg, beaten
50g (2oz) ground almonds
1 teaspoon almond essence

and floured baking tray. Now form
the twist into a circle and pinch the
ends to join and seal them. Loosely
cover the dough with a damp tea
towel and leave it in a warm place to
prove for 45 minutes.

Preheat the oven to 200°C/400°F
/GM 6. Remove the tea towel and
bake the dough in the oven for
25 to 30 minutes, or until
golden and cooked
through.
Carefully
transfer

the twist to a wire rack and leave
it to cool.

Rolling out dough

Maple syrup and pecan

Adding skimmed milk

Adding pecans

Ingredients

1 cup water, tepid
1 tablespoon dried skimmed milk
1 teaspoon salt
6 tablespoons maple syrup
2 cups wholemeal-bread flour
1 cup white-bread flour
1 teaspoon yeast

To finish

100g (3½oz) pecan nuts, roughly chopped

Place the first seven ingredients in the baking pan in the order in which they are listed above. Set the programme to 'BASIC'.

When the cycle indicates, add the pecan nuts.

When the bread has been cooked, transfer it to a wire rack and leave it to cool.

Pecan nuts have a high fat content, 70%, and so should be stored in a cool, dark place and you must observe the use-by-date.

Pecans have a buttery richness that makes them delicious to eat as they are or in suitable recipes.

Maple syrup is made by tapping the sap of a maple tree and then boiling it until it is thick and syrupy.

American Indians used it as a sweetener.

Banana and peanut butter

Mash the bananas with the peanut butter and mix together thoroughly.

Add the ingredients to the baking pan in the order in which they are listed above, but adding the banana and peanut-butter mixture after the salt and before the white-bread flour. Set the programme to 'BASIC'.

When the cycle has been completed, transfer the bread to a wire rack and leave it to cool.

Adding peanut mixture

Ingredients
2 bananas
4 tablespoons crunchy
   peanut butter
1 cup milk, warmed
2 tablespoons butter,
   melted and cooled
2 tablespoons caster sugar
$\frac{1}{2}$ teaspoon salt
$3\frac{1}{2}$ cups white-bread flour
1 teaspoon yeast

This is a perfect teatime bread; children love it for its sweet, nutty flavour. It is a perfect way to use bananas that have become very ripe. You can substitute smooth peanut butter if you wish. Sliced and buttered or toasted, the choice is yours.

Honey

Adding buttermilk

Adding honey

Ingredients
$^3/_4$ cup water, tepid
1 medium-sized egg, beaten
$^1/_2$ cup buttermilk
4 tablespoons honey
$^1/_2$ teaspoon salt
$3^1/_4$ cups granary-bread
  flour
1 teaspoon yeast

Place the ingredients in the baking pan in the order in which they are listed above. Set the programme to 'BASIC'.

When the bread has been cooked, transfer it to a wire rack and leave it to cool.

There are so many varieties of honey now available, each with their own distinctive flavour. The variety that you choose to use is up to you, but it must be a runny honey, set honey is not suitable.

Easy vanilla bread

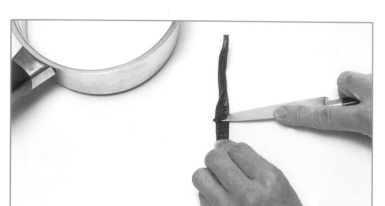

Removing vanilla seeds from pod

Ingredients

1 cup milk

1 vanilla pod

yolks of 2 medium-sized
    eggs, beaten

2 tablespoons butter,
    melted

2 tablespoons buttermilk

5 tablespoons caster sugar

$^1/_2$ teaspoon salt

3 cups white-bread flour

1 teaspoon yeast

Place the milk in a small pan. Using a sharp knife, split the vanilla pod lengthways and add it to the milk. Bring the milk gently to the boil, then remove the pan from the heat and allow the milk to cool until it has just reached body temperature.

Remove the vanilla pod. Using the tip of a knife, scrape the seeds from the vanilla pod and add them to the milk. (Either discard the rest of the vanilla pod or rinse it thoroughly, dry it and then add it to a jar of sugar to make vanilla sugar.)

Whisk together the egg yolks and milk. Now place all of the remaining ingredients in the baking pan. Set the programme to 'BASIC'.

When the cycle has been completed, transfer the bread to a wire rack and leave it to cool.

Chocolate and pear

Place the first eight ingredients in the baking pan in the order in which they are listed above. Set the programme to 'DOUGH'.

Roughly chop the dried pears and place them in a bowl with the coffee. Leave the pear mixture to soak, stirring it from time to time.

Roughly chop the chocolate and then put it to one side.

When the dough is ready, turn it out onto a lightly floured surface and knead it. Divide the dough into two pieces. Taking one of the pieces of dough, press it evenly into the base of a 22cm (8½in) funnel tin. Sprinkle over the soaked pears and the chopped chocolate. Now shape the second piece of dough so that it fits over the pears and

Ingredients
1 cup milk, tepid
1 egg, beaten
4 tablespoons butter, melted and cooled
4 tablespoons caster sugar
½ teaspoon salt
freshly grated zest of 1 lemon
3 cups white-bread flour
1 teaspoon yeast

To finish
150g (5oz) dried, ready-to-eat pears
4 tablespoons strong black coffee, hot
100g (3½oz) good-quality dark chocolate
1 tablespoon cocoa powder, sifted
4 tablespoons icing sugar, sifted

Placing dough into tin

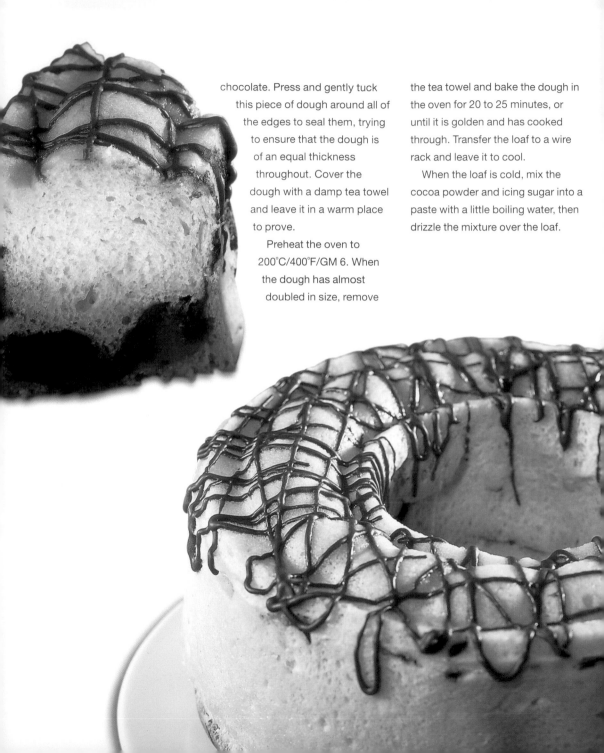

chocolate. Press and gently tuck this piece of dough around all of the edges to seal them, trying to ensure that the dough is of an equal thickness throughout. Cover the dough with a damp tea towel and leave it in a warm place to prove.

Preheat the oven to 200°C/400°F/GM 6. When the dough has almost doubled in size, remove the tea towel and bake the dough in the oven for 20 to 25 minutes, or until it is golden and has cooked through. Transfer the loaf to a wire rack and leave it to cool.

When the loaf is cold, mix the cocoa powder and icing sugar into a paste with a little boiling water, then drizzle the mixture over the loaf.

Stollen

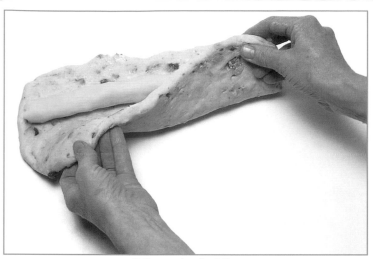

Rolling marzipan for stollen

Ingredients
1 cup milk, warm
3 tablespoons honey
yolks of 2 eggs
$^1/_2$ teaspoon salt
freshly grated zest of 1
 lemon
5 tablespoons butter,
 melted and cooled
$^1/_2$ teaspoon ground mixed
 spice
3 cups white-bread flour
1$^1/_2$ teaspoons yeast

To finish
25g (1oz) currants
50g (2oz) sultanas
50g (2oz) golden raisins
25g (1oz) mixed candied
 peel
25g (1oz) glacé cherries,
 rinsed, dried and coarsely
 chopped
25g (1oz) blanched
 almonds, chopped
300g (11oz) marzipan
icing sugar for dusting

Place the first nine ingredients in the baking pan. Set the programme to 'DOUGH'.

When the programme indicates, add the currants, sultanas, raisins, candied peel, glacé cherries and almonds.

At the end of the cycle, transfer the dough to a lightly floured surface and knead it for 2 to 3 minutes.

Divide the dough in half. Roll out one piece into an oblong measuring approximately 28 x 17.75cm (11 x 7in). Shape half of the marzipan into a sausage shape that is not quite as long as the dough and then place it on the dough. Fold over the long edge of the dough so that the marzipan is enclosed. Press the edges gently together to seal them and then place the dough on a lightly greased and floured baking tray. Repeat this procedure with the remaining dough and marzipan. Loosely cover the dough with a damp tea towel and leave it in a warm place to rise.

Preheat the oven to 200°C/400°F /GM 6. When the dough has almost doubled in size, remove the tea towel and bake the dough in the oven for 20 to 25 minutes, or until the stollen is golden and has cooked through. Transfer the stollen to a wire rack and leave it to cool.

Liberally dust the stollen with icing sugar before serving.

Rolling stollen

Spiced-tea loaf

Adding black tea

Place the first ten ingredients in the baking pan. Set the programme to 'BASIC'.

When the cycle indicates, add the sultanas.

At the end of the cycle, transfer the loaf to a wire rack and leave it to cool.

The loaf tastes delicious plain, but you can ice it if desired.

Ingredients
1 cup black tea, tepid
1 egg, beaten
$\frac{1}{2}$ teaspoon salt
2 tablespoons butter, melted and cooled
2 tablespoons black treacle
1 tablespoon honey
2 teaspoons ground mixed spice
2 cups white-bread flour
1 cup wholemeal-bread flour
1 teaspoon yeast

To finish
75g (3oz) sultanas

Adding beaten eggs

Cranberry and currant

Place the first seven ingredients in the baking pan. Set the programme to 'DOUGH'.

When the dough is ready, transfer it to a floured surface. Now knead the cranberries and currants into the dough until they have been evenly dispersed. Divide the dough into 3 equal-sized pieces and then roll each piece into a long sausage shape measuring approximately 30.5cm (12in) in length. Loosely plait together the three lengths of dough, pinching the ends together to seal them. Place the plait on a greased baking sheet, cover it with a piece of oiled clingfilm and leave it to prove in a warm place. Preheat the oven to 200°/400°F/GM 6. When the dough has almost doubled in size, remove the clingfilm and lightly brush the plait with some beaten egg. Bake the plait in the oven for 20 to 25 minutes, or until it is golden. Transfer the plait to a wire rack and leave it to cool before serving it.

Ingredients
1 cup water, tepid
3 tablespoons honey
2 tablespoons butter, melted
$^1/_2$ teaspoon salt
$2^1/_4$ cups white-bread flour
1 cup wholemeal-bread flour
1 teaspoon yeast

To finish
75g (3oz) dried cranberries
75g (3oz) currants
beaten egg for brushing over

Making the plait

Panettone

Adding lemon zest

lemon zest until they have been well incorporated. Press the dough into a well-buttered round, deep cake tin measuring 17.75cm (7in) in diameter. Cover the dough with a piece of oiled clingfilm and leave it to prove in a warm place.

Preheat the oven to 220°C/425°F /GM 7. When the dough has risen, remove the clingfilm and brush the

Pressing dough into tin

Ingredients

$\frac{1}{2}$ cup milk, tepid
$\frac{1}{2}$ cup water, tepid
1 teaspoon caster sugar
2 teaspoons yeast
3 cups white-bread flour
2 tablespoons caster sugar
pinch of salt
yolks of 2 medium-sized
    eggs
75g (3oz) butter, melted
    and cooled

To finish

50g (2oz) mixed peel,
    chopped
100g (3$\frac{1}{2}$oz) raisins
finely grated zest of 1 lemon
beaten egg for brushing
    over

Pour the warmed milk and water into a mixing bowl. Add 1 teaspoon caster sugar, 2 teaspoons yeast and 1 cup of the white-bread flour. Mix the ingredients together and then cover the bowl with a sheet of clingfilm and leave the dough to prove in a warm place for 1 to 2 hours.

When the dough has risen and looks quite bubbly, pour it into the baking pan and add the rest of the white-bread flour, the caster sugar, salt, eggs and butter. Set the programme to 'DOUGH'.

When the dough is ready, transfer it to a lightly floured surface. Now knead in the mixed peel, raisins and

top of the dough with the beaten egg. Bake the dough in the oven for 10 minutes. Now reduce the heat to 180°C/350°F/GM 4 and continue to bake the panettone for 15 minutes, or until it is golden and has cooked through. Transfer the panettone to a wire rack and leave it to cool.

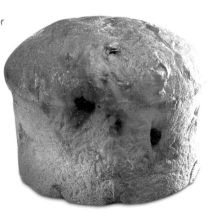

Challah

Adding melted butter

30.5cm (12in) in length. Pinch the top end of each length of dough together, then weave the pieces into a plait. Pinch the bottom ends together, then tuck both ends under the dough to form a neatly plaited

Saffron soaking

Ingredients

pinch of saffron threads
1 tablespoon water, boiling
2 medium-sized eggs, beaten
3 tablespoons honey
$^2/_3$ cup water, tepid
5 tablespoons butter, melted
1 teaspoon salt
$3^1/_2$ cups white-bread flour
$1^1/_2$ teaspoons yeast

To finish

beaten egg for brushing over

In a small bowl, soak the saffron threads in the boiling water for 10 minutes.

Place the beaten eggs in another bowl, then add the saffron and soaking water, the honey, tepid water and melted butter. Mix the ingredients together well. Pour the mixture into the baking pan and then add the salt, flour and yeast. Set the programme to 'DOUGH'.

When the dough is ready, transfer it to a lightly floured surface and knead it for 2 to 3 minutes (it should feel quite soft and silky). Shape the dough into 3 equal-sized pieces, then roll each piece into a sausage shape measuring approximately

loaf. Place the dough on a greased baking tray, cover it with a piece of oiled clingfilm and leave it to prove in a warm place.

Preheat the oven to 220°C/425°F /GM 7. When the dough has almost doubled in size, remove the clingfilm, lightly brush the top of the loaf with beaten egg and then bake the loaf in the oven for 20 to 25 minutes, or until it is golden. Transfer the loaf to a wire rack and leave it to cool before serving it.

Orange and almond

Adding ground almonds

Ingredients

1 cup milk, warmed to a
temperature of between
21 and 28°C
1 medium-sized egg, beaten
4 tablespoons butter,
melted
5 tablespoons caster sugar
$^1/_2$ teaspoon salt
3 cups white-bread flour
1 cup ground almonds
freshly grated zest of 1
orange
$1^1/_2$ teaspoons yeast

Place the ingredients in the baking
pan in the order in which they are
listed above. Set the programme to
'BASIC'.

When the cycle has been
completed, transfer the loaf to a wire
rack and leave it to cool.

Adding orange zest

Oranges and almonds
complement each other perfectly
and are often used together in
Middle Eastern cookery.

This makes a perfect teatime
bread that is good with butter
and jams.

If you have a few stale slices left,
make French toast by dipping the
slices in a mixture of beaten egg and
milk and then frying until golden
brown on each side.

Sprinkle with a little sugar and
serve.

Chocolate

Into a bowl, sift together the white-bread flour, cocoa and cinnamon.

Place the ingredients in the baking pan in the order in which they are listed above, adding the flour mixture after the salt and before the yeast. Set the programme to 'BASIC'.

When the cycle has been completed, transfer the loaf to a wire rack and leave it to cool.

A dark chocolatey bread that is good buttered, or try it with your favourite fruit jam.

The addition of cinnamon brings out the flavour of the chocolate without other sweetening.

As an alternative to cinnamon you could use a teaspoon of fine coffee powder to make more of a mocha flavour.

Sieving in cocoa

Ingredients

2 ³/₄ cups white-bread flour
¹/₄ cup cocoa powder
1 teaspoon ground cinnamon
1 cup milk, warmed to a temperature of between 21 and 28°C
1 medium-sized egg, beaten
1 tablespoon butter, melted
4 tablespoons honey
¹/₂ teaspoon salt
1 teaspoon yeast

Malt loaf

Adding treacle

In a mixing bowl, whisk together the egg and milk, then add all of the ingredients to the baking pan. Set the programme to 'BASIC'.

When the cycle indicates, add the sultanas.

When the cycle has finished, transfer the loaf to a wire rack and leave it to cool for 20 minutes before serving it.

A dark sweet loaf that is delicious with butter. This loaf is not as sticky and dense as the commercially produced loaf of the same name, but very tasty none the less.

Sweetened with honey, treacle and malt it really needs nothing more than a little butter and a cup of tea to make a perfect afternoon snack.

Ingredients

1 egg, beaten
$\frac{1}{2}$ cup milk, warmed to a temperature of between 21 and 28°C
$\frac{1}{2}$ cup water, tepid
1 tablespoon honey
2 tablespoons malt extract
1 tablespoon black treacle
$\frac{1}{2}$ teaspoon salt
3 cups white-bread flour
1 teaspoon yeast

To finish

75g (3oz) sultanas

Toffee and apple

Adding filling

Place the first seven ingredients in the baking pan in the order in which they are listed above. Set the programme to 'DOUGH'.

In a mixing bowl, combine the apple pieces with the butter and brown sugar and then set the bowl to one side.

When the dough is ready, transfer it to a floured surface and knead it briefly. Using a rolling pin, roll out the dough into an oblong measuring approximately 51 x 25.5cm (20 x 10in). Spread the apple and butter mixture over the dough to within 2.5cm (1in) of the edges. Sprinkle the cinnamon evenly over the apple mixture.

Taking one of the long ends, roll up the dough as you would a swiss roll. Pinch all of the edges well to seal them. Carefully transfer the dough to a lightly oiled and floured baking sheet, cover it with a sheet of oiled clingfilm and leave it to prove in a warm place for 35 minutes, or until it has almost doubled in size.

Preheat the oven to 200°C/400°F /GM 6. Using a sharp, dampened knife, make small slashes at regular intervals across the top of the dough. Bake the dough in the oven for 25 minutes, or until it is golden and has cooked through.

In the meantime, gently heat the milk and caster sugar in a small pan until the sugar has dissolved. Continue to cook the sugar-and-milk mixture for 1 minute, then remove the pan from the heat.

When the loaf is ready, transfer it to a wire rack, liberally brush it with the sugar-and-milk mixture and then leave to cool a little.

This bread can be served either warm or cold.

Ingredients

$^1/_2$ cup water, tepid
$^1/_2$ cup milk, warmed
1 tablespoon soft, dark-brown sugar
1 teaspoon salt
3 tablespoons butter, melted and cooled
$3^1/_4$ cups white-bread flour
1 teaspoon yeast

To finish

4 eating apples, peeled, cored and chopped
25g (1oz) butter, melted and cooled
50g (2oz) soft, dark-brown sugar
2 teaspoons ground cinnamon
3 tablespoons milk
1 tablespoon caster sugar

ROLLS, BUNS

&

SNACKS

Coriander rice naans

Place the first seven ingredients in the baking pan and set the programme to 'DOUGH'.

Mix the rice and coriander with the melted butter and season to taste with the salt and pepper.

When the bleep sounds, add the rice, butter and coriander mixture. When the cycle has been completed, remove the dough.

Knead the dough briefly and then divide it into 9 equal-sized pieces. With floured hands, shape each piece into a large, flat, teardrop shape. Leave the pieces to rest for 10 minutes.

Heat a heavy-based frying pan over a moderately high heat, then cook the naans in batches for 4 to 5 minutes or until they start to turn golden in places, turning each naan halfway through.

Either serve the naans warm or allow them to cool before wrapping them in foil. Reheat them in a hot oven for 5 minutes.

Ingredients
1 cup water, tepid
2 tablespoons dried skimmed milk
1 tablespoon honey
1 teaspoon ground cumin
1 teaspoon salt
3 cups white-bread flour
1 teaspoon yeast

To finish
1½ cups cold, cooked basmati rice
3 tablespoons fresh coriander, chopped
2 tablespoons butter, melted
salt
freshly ground black pepper

Rolling the naans

Muffins

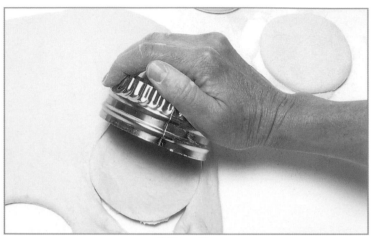

Cutting muffins

Ingredients
1 cup water, tepid
2 tablespoons dried
   skimmed milk
2 teaspoons honey
3 tablespoons butter,
   melted
$^1/_2$ teaspoon salt
$3^1/_4$ cups white-bread flour
1 teaspoon yeast

To finish
fine cornmeal

Place the first seven ingredients in the baking pan in the order in which they are listed above. Set the programme to 'DOUGH'.

When the cycle has been completed, remove the dough and knead it on a lightly floured surface for 2 to 3 minutes.

Using a rolling pin, roll out the dough to a thickness of about 1.30cm ($^1/_2$in). Using a 10cm (4in) round cutter, stamp out rounds. Knead together any remaining bits of dough. Repeat the rolling, stamping and kneading until all the dough has been used up. Dust the muffins with the fine cornmeal and leave them to rest for 10 minutes.

Heat a heavy-based frying pan (preferably made of cast iron) over a moderately high heat and then cook the muffins in batches for about 7 minutes, turning each muffin halfway through.

Either split and butter the muffins and serve them immediately or allow them to cool on a wire rack before splitting and toasting them.

Pikelets

Turning pikelets

Ingredients
$^1/_2$ cup water, tepid
$^1/_2$ cup milk, tepid
1 egg, beaten
1 teaspoon caster sugar
$^1/_2$ teaspoon salt
$1^1/_4$ cups white-bread flour
1 teaspoon yeast

Place all of the ingredients in the baking pan in the order in which they are listed above. Set the programme to 'DOUGH'.

When the cycle has been completed, remove the baking pan. Heat a heavy-based frying pan over a moderately high heat. When the frying pan is hot, pour a tablespoon of the runny mixture into the pan so that it forms a small pancake. Cook the pancake until the top has set, then turn it over using a palette knife and cook it for a further 1 or 2 minutes, until golden spots start to appear.

Repeat the process until all of the mixture has been used up.

Butter the pikelets and serve them warm. Alternatively, you could leave them to cool and reheat them under the grill.

Honey and thyme knots

Knotting the dough

knots with a sheet of lightly oiled clingfilm and leave them in a warm place to prove.

Preheat the oven to 200°C/400°F /GM 6. When the knots have almost doubled in size, remove the clingfilm, drizzle each knot with honey and scatter over a few thyme leaves. Bake in the oven for 20 minutes, or until the knots have turned golden. Transfer the knots to a wire rack and leave them to cool.

Ingredients
1 cup water, tepid
1 teaspoon salt
3 tablespoons honey
2 tablespoons sunflower oil
2 tablespoons fresh thyme
  leaves
3 cups white-bread flour
$\frac{1}{4}$ cup wheatgerm
$1\frac{1}{2}$ teaspoons yeast

To finish
2 tablespoons honey
1 tablespoon fresh thyme
  leaves

Place the first eight ingredients in the baking pan in the order in which they are listed above. Set the programme to 'DOUGH'.

At the end of the cycle, remove the dough, transfer it to a lightly floured surface and knead it for 2 to 3 minutes. Divide the mixture into 9 equal-sized pieces. Working with one piece at a time, roll the dough into a sausage shape about 20.5cm (8in) long and tie it into a knot before placing it on a lightly oiled and floured baking tray. Repeat the process with each piece of dough. Loosely cover the

Pancetta-wrapped pesto rolls

Wrapping the pancetta

Place the first six ingredients in the baking pan in the order in which they are listed above. Set the programme to 'DOUGH'.

When the cycle has been completed, transfer the dough to a lightly floured surface and knead it for 2 to 3 minutes. Using a lightly floured rolling pin, roll out the dough into a rectangle measuring approximately 51 x 15.25cm (20 x 6in). Spread the rectangle with the pesto. Taking one of the long edges, roll up the dough so that the pesto is enclosed and then pinch the edge to seal it. Using a sharp knife, cut the dough into 8 equal-sized pieces and then loosely wrap a slice of pancetta around each roll. Place the rolls on a lightly oiled baking tray, loosely cover them with a sheet of oiled clingfilm and leave them in a warm place to prove.

Preheat the oven to 200°C/400°F /GM 6. When the rolls have almost doubled in size, remove the clingfilm and bake them in the oven for 15 minutes, or until they are golden and the pancetta is crisp. Transfer the rolls to a wire rack and leave them to cool.

These rolls are best eaten on the day that you make them.

Ingredients
$^1/_2$ cup water, tepid
$^1/_2$ teaspoon salt
1 teaspoon honey
1 tablespoon olive oil
1 $^3/_4$ cups white-bread flour
$^1/_2$ teaspoon yeast

To finish
3 tablespoons good-quality pesto
8 thin slices pancetta

Dog biscuits

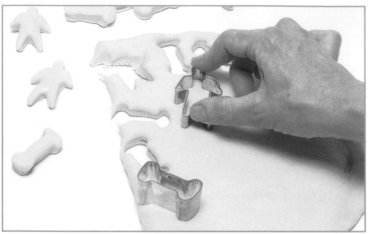

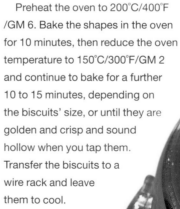

Cutting out the shapes

Ingredients
1 cup chicken stock,
   warmed to a temperature
   of 21 to 28°C
2 tablespoons dried
   skimmed milk
2 tablespoons olive oil
$^1/_2$ teaspoon salt
1 egg, beaten
2 cups white-bread flour
$1^1/_2$ cups plain brown flour
1 teaspoon yeast

Place all of the ingredients in the baking pan in the order in which they are listed above. Set the programme to 'DOUGH'.

When the cycle has finished, transfer the dough to a floured surface and knead it briefly. Using a lightly floured rolling pin, roll out the dough to a thickness of 1.3cm ($^1/_2$in). Then, using a cookie cutter of your choice, cut out shapes from the dough and place them on a lightly floured baking tray. Re-roll any scraps of dough and continue cutting and rolling it until all of the dough has been used up. Leave the shapes to rest for 20 minutes.

Preheat the oven to 200°C/400°F /GM 6. Bake the shapes in the oven for 10 minutes, then reduce the oven temperature to 150°C/300°F/GM 2 and continue to bake for a further 10 to 15 minutes, depending on the biscuits' size, or until they are golden and crisp and sound hollow when you tap them. Transfer the biscuits to a wire rack and leave them to cool.

When the biscuits are completely cold, store them in an airtight container.

Danish pastries

Ingredients
1 cup water, tepid
3 tablespoons dried
    skimmed milk
2 eggs, beaten
2 tablespoons caster sugar
$^1/_2$ teaspoon salt
$3^1/_2$ cups white-bread flour
1 teaspoon yeast

To finish
250g (9oz) unsalted butter
1 x 425g (15oz) tin apricot
    halves, drained
1 egg, beaten
50g (2oz) icing sugar
25g (1oz) flaked almonds,
    toasted

Place the first seven ingredients in the baking pan in the order in which they are listed above. Set the programme to 'DOUGH'.

Place the butter between 2 sheets of greaseproof paper and, using a rolling pin, beat it into a square approximately 1.3cm ($^1/_2$in) thick. Cover and chill.

When the cycle has been completed, transfer the dough to a well-floured surface and knead it briefly. Now roll out the dough so that it is approximately 2cm ($^3/_4$in) wider than your sheet of butter and half as long again. Unwrap the chilled butter and lay it on the dough, leaving a small border of dough on three sides at one end. Fold the top piece of dough, the part that has not been used, over half of the butter, then fold the bottom piece of butter and dough up and over it. (You have now folded the butter and dough into three layers, rather like folding a letter.) Seal the open edges with a rolling pin, then give the dough a quarter turn to the left (the completely enclosed side should always be on the left) and repeat the rolling-and-folding

Making an apricot Danish step 1

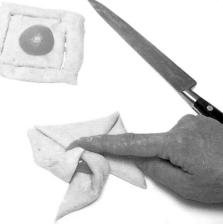

189

process once more. Place the dough on a lightly floured plate, cover it with clingfilm and chill for 30 minutes. Repeat the rolling-and-folding process twice more, then chill the dough for another 30 minutes.

Now roll out the dough to a thickness of about 5mm ($^1/_4$in), trim the edges and, using a sharp knife, cut it into 10cm (4in) squares. Place a drained apricot half, cut side down, in the centre of each square, then cut the dough to shape.

To make a pinwheel: using a sharp knife, make four cuts, running from the apricot to each corner of the dough, and then brush on some of the beaten egg. Taking alternate corners of the dough, fold the points inwards, onto the apricot, pinching them firmly to seal them. Repeat the process for each pastry.

To make a fold-over: using the tip of a sharp knife, cut the dough 1.3cm ($^1/_2$in) from the edge on two sides, making sure that you start and finish 1.3cm ($^1/_2$in) away from the corners. Repeat this process on the other side. (You now should have a square within a square whose opposite corners have not been cut through.) Brush on some more of the beaten egg. Taking one

cut side, fold it over so that it rests on the opposite side within the inner square. Repeat the process with the other cut edge. Now repeat the fold-over process for each pastry.

Transfer the pastries to a lightly greased and floured baking tray, allowing room for each piece to rise. Loosely cover the pastries with a damp tea towel and leave them to prove at room temperature for 45 minutes. (Do not leave them in too warm a place in case the dough is spoiled.)

Preheat the oven to 200°C/400°F /GM 6. Remove the tea towel and brush each pastry with a little more beaten egg. Transfer the pastries to the oven and bake them for 15 to 20 minutes, or until they are golden and crisp. Transfer the pastries to a wire rack and leave them to cool.

Sieve the icing sugar into a small mixing bowl and then mix in enough boiling water to make a thin icing. When the pastries have cooled, drizzle them with the icing and sprinkle over the almonds.

Making an apricot Danish step 2

Icing the apricot Danish step 3

Pain au raisin

Place the first seven ingredients in the baking pan in the order in which they are listed above. Set the programme to 'DOUGH'.

Place the butter between 2 sheets of greaseproof paper and then, using a rolling pin, beat it into a square approximately 1cm (¹/₂in) thick. Cover and chill.

When the cycle has been completed, transfer the dough to a well-floured surface and knead it briefly. Now roll out the dough so that it is approximately 2cm (³/₄in) wider than your sheet of butter and half as long again. Unwrap the chilled butter and lay it on one end of the dough, leaving a small border of dough on three sides. Taking the top piece of dough (the piece that has not been used), fold it over half of the butter, then fold the bottom piece of dough up over it. (You

should now have folded the butter and dough into three layers, like folding a letter.) Seal the open edges with a rolling pin, then give the dough a quarter turn to the left (the completely enclosed side should always be on the left) and repeat the rolling-and-folding process once more. Place the dough on a lightly floured plate, cover it with clingfilm and chill it for 30 minutes.

Repeat the rolling-and-folding process twice more, then chill the dough for 30 minutes.

Roll the dough into an oblong measuring approximately 56 x 25.5cm (22 x 10in). Sprinkle over the raisins and caster sugar, then take one of the long edges and roll up the dough so that the filling is enclosed, pinching the finished edge to seal it. Wrap a piece of fine string around the dough, about 1.3cm (¹/₂in) from the

Ingredients
³/₄ cup water, tepid
3 tablespoons unsalted
  butter, melted and cooled
2 eggs, beaten
1 tablespoon honey
1 teaspoon salt
3 cups white-bread flour
1 teaspoon yeast

To finish
250g (9oz) unsalted butter
200g (7oz) raisins
2 tablespoons caster sugar
4 tablespoons apricot jam
1 tablespoon water

Rolling raisins in dough

191

end, pull it gently to cut through the dough and place the slice of dough cut side up on a lightly greased and floured baking tray, allowing room for each piece to rise.

Continue this procedure until all of the dough has been used up. Loosely cover the dough pieces with a damp tea towel and leave them to prove at room temperature. Preheat the oven to 200°C/400°F /GM 6.

To make the apricot glaze: place the apricot jam and 1 tablespoon of water in a small pan and heat it gently while stirring the mixture. When the water has been well incorporated into the jam, remove the pan from the heat and strain the mixture through a sieve into a bowl. Set to one side.

When the pain au raisin have puffed up to half their size again, remove the tea towel and bake them in the oven for 15 to 20 minutes, or until they are golden and crisp. As soon as you take them out of the oven, transfer them to a wire rack, brush them liberally with the apricot-jam glaze and leave them to cool.

The pain au raisin are best eaten on the day of making. Alternatively, reheat them for 5 minutes before serving them.

Tie string around one end

Pull the string to cut

Cherry and custard fold-overs

Place the first seven ingredients in the baking pan in the order in which they are listed above. Set the programme to 'DOUGH'.

Place the butter between 2 sheets of greaseproof paper. Using a rolling pin, beat the butter into a square approximately 1.3cm ($^1/_2$in) thick. Cover and chill.

When the cycle has been completed, transfer the dough to a well-floured surface and knead it briefly. Now roll out the dough so that it is approximately 2cm ($^3/_4$in) wider than your sheet of butter and half as long again.

Unwrap the chilled butter and lay it on the dough, leaving a small border of dough on three sides at one end. Fold the top piece of dough, the part that has not been used, over half of the butter. then

Ingredients
1 cup water, tepid
3 tablespoons dried skimmed milk
2 eggs, beaten
2 tablespoons caster sugar
$^1/_2$ teaspoon salt
$3^1/_2$ cups white-bread flour
1 teaspoon yeast

To finish
250g (9oz) unsalted butter
1 x 425g (15oz) tin black cherries, pitted and drained
$^1/_2$ pint ready-made thick custard
1 egg, beaten
icing sugar for dusting

fold the bottom piece of butter and dough up and over it. (You have now folded the butter and dough into three layers, rather like folding a letter.) Seal the open edges with a rolling pin, then give the dough a quarter turn to the left (the completely enclosed side should always be on the left) and repeat the rolling-and-folding process once more. Place the dough on a lightly floured plate, cover it with clingfilm and chill for 30 minutes.

Repeat the rolling-and-folding process twice more, then chill the dough for another 30 minutes.

Now roll out the dough to a thickness of about 5mm ($^1/_4$in), trim the edges and, using a sharp knife, cut it into oblongs measuring approximately 10 x 15.25cm (4 x 6in). Divide the cherries and custard between each piece, making sure that the filling does not go beyond 1.3cm ($^1/_2$in) of the edges. Brush the edges of each piece with a little beaten egg, then fold over the longer edge so that it encloses the filling. Pinch the edges firmly to seal them.

Place the fold-overs on a lightly greased and floured baking tray (or more if necessary), allowing room between them for each to rise. Loosely cover the fold-overs with a sheet of oiled clingfilm and leave

them to prove at room temperature for 30 minutes.

Preheat the oven to 200°C/400°F /GM 6. Remove the clingfilm and brush each fold-over with a little more beaten egg. Bake in the oven for 15 to 20 minutes, or until the fold-overs are golden and crisp. Finally, dust with icing sugar.

The fold-overs may be eaten hot or cold.

Cheese and onion

Adding cayenne pepper

Ingredients

1 cup water, tepid
1 tablespoon dried skimmed
  milk
1 teaspoon salt
1 teaspoon caster sugar
1 tablespoon sunflower oil
$\frac{1}{2}$ teaspoon dried thyme
$\frac{1}{2}$ teaspoon dried oregano
$\frac{1}{4}$ teaspoon cayenne pepper
$3\frac{1}{4}$ cups white-bread flour
1 teaspoon yeast

To finish

1 small onion, peeled and
  very finely chopped
125g ($4\frac{1}{2}$oz) mature
  Cheddar cheese, grated
milk for glazing

Place the first ten ingredients in the baking pan. Set the programme to 'DOUGH'.

When the cycle indicates, add the onion and 100g ($3\frac{1}{2}$ oz) of the Cheddar cheese.

When the cycle has been completed, transfer the dough to a well-floured surface. Knead the dough briefly (if it is quite wet, knead in a bit of extra flour). Now divide the dough into 7 equal-sized pieces. Shape each piece into a ball and place six balls

197

Adding cheese

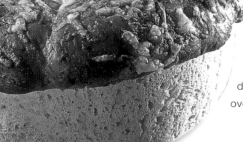

around the edge of a round cake tin, 20.5cm (8in) in diameter. Place the last ball of dough in the centre, cover the cake tin with a piece of oiled clingfilm and leave the dough to prove for 45 minutes, or until it has almost doubled in size. Preheat the oven to 200°C/400°F/GM 6.

Brush the surface of the dough with a little milk, sprinkle over the remaining cheese and then bake the dough in the oven for 25 to 30 minutes, or until it is golden.

Allow the balls to cool for 20 minutes before serving them.

198

Doughnuts

Ingredients

⅝ cup water, tepid

3 tablespoons dried
   skimmed milk

4 tablespoons butter,
   melted and cooled

1 egg, beaten

½ teaspoon salt

2 tablespoons caster sugar

3 cups white-bread flour

1½ teaspoons yeast

To finish

oil for deep-frying

caster sugar for coating

150ml (¼ pint) chocolate
   custard or jam of your
   choice

Place the first eight ingredients in the baking pan in the order in which they are listed above. Set the programme to 'DOUGH'.

When the cycle has finished, transfer the dough to a floured surface and knead it briefly. Now divide the dough into 9 equal-sized pieces. Form each piece into a ball shape and place the balls on a lightly floured baking tray. Loosely cover the balls with a sheet of oiled clingfilm and leave them in a warm place to prove for 30 minutes.

Heat the oil in a deep-fat fryer until it has reached a temperature of 180°C/350°F, then cook the doughnuts in batches for about 2 minutes on each side until they are golden and crisp.

Drain the doughnuts on pieces of kitchen paper, then toss them in the caster sugar. Finally, using a chopstick or thick skewer, make a hole in each doughnut, taking care that it does not go right through the doughnut, and pipe in the chocolate custard or jam.

Squeezing filling into doughnuts

201

Lahmachun

Place the first six ingredients in the baking pan in the order in which they are listed above. Set the programme to 'DOUGH'.

In a frying pan, fry the onion in the oil, then add the chilli powder and cumin and cook for 1 minute. Now add the minced beef and continue to cook, stirring constantly to break down the pieces. When the beef is brown all over, add the chopped tomatoes. Continue to cook over a gentle heat until the mixture has thickened, then remove the pan from the heat. Stir in the coriander and season to taste. Leave the mixture to cool.

Preheat the oven to 200°C/400°F /GM 6. When the dough is ready, transfer it to a lightly floured surface and knead it for 2 minutes. Divide the dough into 8 equal-sized pieces and shape each piece into a ball. Using a lightly floured rolling pin, roll each ball into a round measuring approximately 30.5cm (12in) across, making it as thin as possible. Divide the beef mixture between each round of dough, spreading it thinly to within 1.3cm (¹/₂in) of the edge.

Transfer the dough discs to as many lightly floured baking trays as necessary and cook them in the oven for 6 to 8 minutes, or until they are just starting to turn golden in places at the edges.

Lahmachun can be served hot or cold and are often rolled up and eaten using one's fingers.

Ingredients

1 cup water, tepid
2 tablespoons olive oil
1 teaspoon salt
2 teaspoons honey
3 cups white-bread flour
1 teaspoon yeast

To finish

1 small onion, finely chopped
1 tablespoon olive oil
1 teaspoon mild chilli powder
1 teaspoon ground cumin
200g (7oz) minced beef
1 x 200g (7oz) tin chopped tomatoes
2 tablespoons fresh coriander, chopped
salt and pepper to taste

Rolling out dough

Bacon and cheese

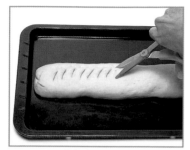

Snipping the top

Preheat the oven to 200°C/400°F /GM 6. When the dough has almost doubled in size, remove the tea towel. Using a pair of kitchen scissors, make a series of cuts in the top of each roll. Bake the rolls in the oven for 15 to 20 minutes, or until golden and crisp. Transfer the rolls to a wire rack and allow them to cool for 10 minutes.

Slice the rolls and serve them immediately.

Ingredients

3/4 cup water, tepid
2 tablespoons dried skimmed milk
1 tablespoon sunflower oil
1 teaspoon caster sugar
1/2 teaspoon salt
2 3/4 cups white-bread flour
1 teaspoon yeast

To finish

6 rashers smoked, streaky bacon, cooked until crispy
100g (3 1/2 oz) grated red Leicester cheese

Place the first seven ingredients in the baking pan in the order in which they are listed above. Set the programme to 'DOUGH'.

When the cycle has finished, transfer the dough to a floured surface and knead it briefly. Using a lightly floured rolling pin, roll out the dough into an oblong measuring approximately 51 x 23cm (20 x 9in). Crumble the bacon into small pieces and sprinkle them over the length of the dough, followed by the grated cheese.

Taking one of the long edges, roll up the dough so that the filling is enclosed and then pinch the edges to seal them. Cut the dough in half, place the two rolls on a lightly greased and floured baking tray and cover them with a damp tea towel. Leave them in a warm place to prove.

Double corn

Adding sweetcorn

Preheat the oven to 200°C/400°F /GM 6. Remove the clingfilm and bake the tins in the oven for 20 minutes, or until the bread is golden. After about 5 minutes, carefully remove the bread rolls from the tins, transfer them to a wire rack and leave them to cool.

Note

This bread can also be made from start to finish in the bread-maker. If you would prefer to do this, just set the programme to 'BASIC'. The reason why I cooked it in tin cans is because this is a traditional way to bake corn bread.

Ingredients

1 cup water, tepid
1 tablespoon sunflower oil
$\frac{1}{2}$ cup buttermilk
1 teaspoon honey
1 teaspoon salt
3 cups white-bread flour
1 cup fine cornmeal
1 teaspoon yeast

To finish

$\frac{1}{2}$ cup corn kernels, cooked
and thoroughly drained
$\frac{1}{2}$ teaspoon chilli powder

Place the first nine ingredients in the baking pan in the order in which they are listed above. Set the programme to 'DOUGH'.

When indicated, add the corn kernels and chilli powder.

When the cycle has finished, transfer the dough to a floured surface and knead it for 2 to 3 minutes. You will now need 8 empty 425g (15oz) tin cans that have been cleaned and thoroughly oiled. Divide the dough between the 8 tins, taking care not to cut yourself on the sharp edges. Cover the tins with a sheet of oiled clingfilm and leave them to prove until the dough has almost doubled in size.

Left: Made as the recipe suggests in tin cans

Right: Made entirely in the bread machine on BASIC

Mustard sausage rolls

Adding tomato ketchup

Ingredients

$3/4$ cup water, tepid
1 tablespoon sunflower oil
3 tablespoons tomato
  ketchup
1 teaspoon salt
3 tablespoons fine cornmeal
$2^{1}/2$ cups white-bread flour
1 teaspoon yeast

To finish

2 tablespoons sunflower oil
1 large onion, peeled and
  thinly sliced
8 good-quality sausages
mustard

Place the first seven ingredients in the baking pan in the order in which they are listed above. Set the programme to 'DOUGH'.

In a large frying pan, heat the sunflower oil and gently cook the onions until they are transparent and starting to turn golden brown in places. Using a slotted spoon, remove the onions and put them to one side to cool. Now cook the sausages in the same pan. When the sausages are cooked, remove them from the pan and set them to one side to cool.

When the cycle has finished, transfer the dough to a floured surface and knead it briefly. Divide the dough into 8 equal-sized pieces. Taking one piece of dough, press and stretch it until it is big enough to enclose a sausage. Smear a little mustard down the centre of the dough and then top the mustard with an eighth of the onions, followed by one of the sausages. Draw up the dough to enclose the filling and pinch the edges together to seal them. Place the sausage roll, seam side down, on a lightly oiled baking sheet and loosely cover it with a sheet of oiled clingfilm. Using the remaining dough and filling, repeat this procedure until you have eight sausage rolls. Leave the sausage rolls to prove at room temperature for 45 minutes.

Preheat the oven to 200°C/400°F /GM 6. Remove the clingfilm and bake the sausage rolls in the oven for 20 to 25 minutes, or until they are golden brown and piping hot. Transfer the sausage rolls to a wire rack and allow them to cool for 10 minutes.

Serve immediately.

Folding the hot dogs

Teacakes

Shaping the dough

teacake on a lightly oiled and greased baking tray, allowing enough room between them for each to rise. Loosely cover the teacakes with a damp tea towel and leave them to prove at room temperature (the temperature should not be too warm because the texture of the teacakes benefits from a longer, slower rise).

Preheat the oven to 200°C/400°F /GM 6. When the teacakes have almost doubled in size, remove the tea towel and brush each teacake with milk. Bake the teacakes in the oven for approximately 20 minutes, or until they are golden. Transfer the teacakes to a wire rack and sieve a light dusting of flour over each of them. Cover the teacakes with a dry tea towel and leave them to cool.

Split and toast the teacakes before serving them.

Ingredients
½ cup black tea, tepid
½ cup milk, warmed
2 tablespoons butter, melted and cooled
2 tablespoons caster sugar
½ teaspoon salt
3 cups white-bread flour
1 teaspoon yeast

To finish
100g (3½ oz) mixed sultanas and raisins
25g (1oz) chopped mixed peel
milk for brushing
flour for dusting

Place the first seven ingredients in the baking pan in the order in which they are listed above. Set the programme to 'DOUGH'.

When indicated, add the sultanas and raisins and mixed peel.

At the end of the cycle, transfer the dough to a floured surface and knead it briefly. Divide the dough into 8 equal-sized pieces and then shape each piece into a round about 2 cm (³/₄in) thick. Place each

210

Hot cross buns

Creating the cross

Ingredients
1 medium-sized egg, beaten
1 cup milk, warmed to a
  temperature of between
  21 and 28°C
4 tablespoons butter,
  melted and cooled
4 tablespoons caster sugar
$1/2$ teaspoon salt
2 teaspoons ground mixed
  spice
$3^1/4$ cups white-bread flour
2 teaspoons yeast

To finish
100g ($3^1/2$ oz) currants
50g (2oz) mixed candied
  peel
2 tablespoons plain flour
3 tablespoons caster sugar
3 tablespoons milk

Whisk together the egg, milk and butter, then place the mixture in the baking pan. Now add the following five ingredients in the order in which they are listed above, ending with the yeast. Set the programme to 'DOUGH'.

When the cycle indicates, add the currants and candied peel.

When the dough is ready, transfer it to a floured surface and knead for 1 to 2 minutes. Divide the dough into 8 equal-sized pieces and then form each piece into a ball. Place the buns on a greased baking tray, allowing enough room between them for them to rise. Cover the buns with a piece of oiled clingfilm and leave them to prove at room temperature (allowing them to rise gently improves their texture).

In a mixing bowl, mix the flour with 1 tablespoon of the caster sugar and add enough water to make a stiff paste. Heat the milk and the remaining caster sugar in a pan until the sugar has dissolved. Preheat the oven to 200°C/400°F /GM 6. When the buns have almost doubled in size, remove the clingfilm. Using a scalpel or a very sharp knife, lightly mark a cross into the top of

each bun. Transfer the flour-and-sugar paste to a piping bag and, using the cross as a guideline, pipe a cross of paste onto each bun.

Bake the buns in the oven for 15 to 20 minutes, or until they are golden and have cooked through. Remove the buns from the oven and transfer them to a wire rack. Brush the top of each with the sugar-and-milk glaze and leave them to cool.

Hot cross buns are best served either warm or toasted.

Adding ground mixed spices

Cheese and Marmite twists

Lightly press ends together

Ingredients

1 cup water, tepid
1 tablespoon skimmed milk
 powder
2 tablespoons olive oil
1 teaspoon caster sugar
1 teaspoon salt
3 cups white-bread flour
1 teaspoon yeast

To finish

1 tablespoon Marmite
 mixed with 1 teaspoon
 water
125g (4½oz) Cheddar
 cheese, grated
1 egg, beaten

Place the first seven ingredients in the baking pan in the order in which they are listed above. Set the programme to 'DOUGH'.

When the cycle has been completed, transfer the dough to a lightly floured surface and knead it for 2 to 3 minutes. Using a floured rolling pin, roll out the dough into a rectangle measuring approximately 51 x 63.5cm (20 x 25in). Spread the Marmite over half of the dough and then sprinkle the cheese over the Marmite. Lightly brush the remaining dough with the beaten egg and fold this

Making the twists

section over the cheese and
Marmite section. Using the rolling
pin, press down well to seal the
edges. Using a sharp knife, cut the
dough into thin strips. Divide the
strips between two well-greased
baking trays, twisting them as
you lay them down. Cover the
dough with a sheet of lightly
oiled clingfilm and leave it to
prove in a warm place for about
45 minutes.

Preheat the oven to 200°C/400°F
/GM 6. When the dough has risen
to almost twice its size, bake it in
the oven for 15 to 20 minutes or
until the twists are golden and
crisp. Transfer the twists to a wire
rack and leave them to cool.

Garlic rolls

Ingredients

$^{3}/_{4}$ cups water, tepid
1 tablespoon garlic-
   flavoured oil
1 egg, beaten
1 teaspoon salt
3 cups white-bread flour
1 teaspoon yeast

To finish

1 clove garlic, crushed
2 tablespoons fresh parsley,
   chopped
50g (2oz) butter
beaten egg for brushing
   over

Place the first six ingredients in the baking pan in the order in which they are listed above. Set the programme to 'DOUGH'.

In a mixing bowl, mix together the garlic, parsley and butter.

At the end of the cycle, transfer the dough to a floured surface, knead and then divide and shape it into 8 rounds. Firmly press your thumb into the centre of each round to make an indentation. Divide the butter mixture between each of these indentations, then pinch together the edges of the dough to seal in the butter. Place the rolls on a greased baking tray in two rows, allowing room between them for each one to rise. Loosely cover the rolls with a piece of oiled clingfilm and leave them to prove in a warm place until they have nearly doubled in size.

Preheat the oven to 220°C/425°F /GM 7. Remove the clingfilm and brush each roll with a little beaten egg. Bake the rolls in the oven for 15 to 20 minutes.

These rolls are best served warm.

Adding butter mixture

Walnut and olive

Adding olives and walnuts

Ingredients
1 cup water, tepid
1 tablespoon olive oil
1 tablespoon dried skimmed milk
1 tablespoon honey
1 teaspoon salt
3 cups white-bread flour
1 $\frac{1}{2}$ teaspoons yeast

To finish
100g (3 $\frac{1}{2}$ oz) black olives, pitted and roughly chopped
75g (3oz) walnuts, roughly chopped

Place the first seven ingredients in the baking pan in the order in which they are listed above. Set the programme to 'DOUGH'.

When the cycle has been completed, transfer the dough to a lightly floured surface and knead in the olives and walnuts. When the olives and walnuts have been evenly incorporated, divide the dough into 12 equal-sized pieces. Lightly oil a deep 12-hole muffin pan and place a piece of dough in each hole. Loosely cover the dough with a sheet of lightly oiled clingfilm and leave it in a warm place to prove.

Preheat the oven to 200°C/400°F /GM 6. When the dough has puffed up and has almost doubled in size, remove the clingfilm and bake the dough in the oven for 20 minutes, or until it is golden and crisp. Transfer the rolls to a wire rack and leave them to cool.

220

Apricot twists

Place the first seven ingredients in the baking pan. Set the programme to 'DOUGH'.

Roughly chop the apricots and then combine them with the orange juice in a small pan. Set the pan over a gentle heat and cook the apricots and orange juice for approximately 10 minutes, stirring occasionally, or until the apricots are hot and most of the juice has been absorbed. Tip the apricot mixture into a bowl and set it aside to cool.

When the cycle has been completed, transfer the dough to a well-floured surface and knead it briefly. Now start kneading the cooled apricot mixture into the dough (the dough mixture will be a bit sticky, but work quickly, adding a bit more flour if necessary). Divide the mixture into 8 equal-sized pieces and then, using a floured rolling pin, roll each piece into a rough sausage shape measuring approximately 25.5cm (10in) in length. Take one piece, and while holding it in the centre, draw the two ends together and twist them into a short, fat rope. Place the twist on a well-greased baking tray. Repeat the process until you have twisted all of

the remaining pieces of dough. Cover the dough with a sheet of oiled clingfilm and leave it to prove.

Preheat the oven to 220°C/425°F /GM 7. Remove the clingfilm and then place the twists in the oven for 10 minutes.

In the meantime, heat the butter and sugar in a small pan until the sugar has dissolved.

When the 10 minutes are up, remove the twists from the oven and brush them with the butter mixture before sprinkling the almonds over the top. Return the twists to the oven for a further 5 to 10 minutes, or until they are golden and cooked. Cool for 15 minutes before serving.

Ingredients
1 cup milk, warmed
4 tablespoons caster sugar
2 tablespoons butter, melted and cooled
1 teaspoon vanilla essence
$\frac{1}{2}$ teaspoon of salt
$3\frac{1}{2}$ cups white-bread flour
$1\frac{1}{2}$ teaspoons yeast

To finish
150g (5oz) dried, ready-to-eat apricots
$\frac{1}{4}$ cup freshly squeezed orange juice
2 tablespoons butter, melted
1 tablespoon caster sugar
50g (2oz) flaked almonds, toasted

Shaping the twists

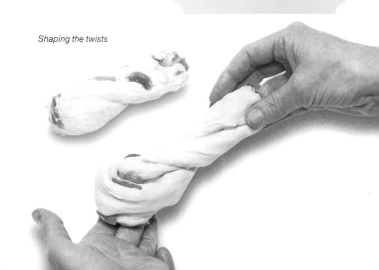

Spiced bread sticks

Adding spice to the breadsticks

baking trays, leaving enough room between each for them to rise. Loosely cover the dough with a sheet of oiled clingfilm and leave it to prove for 30 minutes.

Preheat the oven to 220°C/425°F /GM 7. Remove the clingfilm, brush the bread sticks with the egg-and-water mixture, then sprinkle the spices over the top. Place the breadsticks in the oven and bake them for 10 minutes, or until they are golden and crisp. Transfer the breadsticks to a wire cooling rack and leave them to become cold.

Either enjoy these bread sticks as they are or serve them with dips.

Ingredients
1 cup water, tepid
2 tablespoons sunflower oil
1 teaspoon caster sugar
1 teaspoon salt
$3\frac{1}{4}$ cups white-bread flour
1 teaspoon yeast

To finish
1 teaspoon ground cumin
1 teaspoon ground coriander
1 teaspoon paprika
2 teaspoons celery salt
$\frac{1}{2}$ teaspoon chilli powder
a mix of half egg and water, beaten together

Place the first six ingredients in the baking pan in the order in which they are listed above. Set the programme to 'DOUGH'.

In a small bowl, mix together the cumin, coriander, paprika, celery salt and chilli powder.

When the cycle has finished, transfer the dough to a floured surface and knead it briefly. Using a floured rolling pin, roll out the dough to a thickness of approximately 5mm ($\frac{1}{4}$in) and then cut it into thin strips. With lightly floured hands, roll the strips into thin rounds and place them on lightly greased and floured

Flat breads

Stretching out dough

Place the ingredients in the baking pan in the order in which they are listed above. Set the programme to 'DOUGH'.

When the dough is ready, transfer it to a lightly floured surface. Divide the dough into walnut-sized pieces. Using a lightly floured rolling pin, roll and stretch each ball of dough into a thin disc (the thinner the better because each disc will puff up when cooked).

Warm a large, heavy (preferably cast-iron) frying pan over a high heat. When the pan is almost smoking hot, place the first disc of dough in the pan and cook it for 1 to 2 minutes on each side, using a pair of tongs to turn it over carefully. When the disc has been cooked through, remove it from the pan, cover it with a clean tea towel and keep it warm on top of the oven while you continue the cooking process for the rest of the discs.

Ingredients
1 cup water, tepid
1 teaspoon celery salt
1 tablespoon olive oil
3 cups white-bread flour
1 teaspoon yeast

Either serve these flat breads with Mediterranean- and Middle Eastern-style dishes or use them as wraps to enclose salads and other snacks.

Rolling out

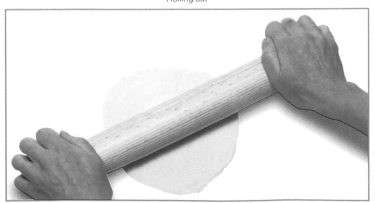

Bagels

Place the first six ingredients in the baking pan in the order in which they are listed above. Set the programme to 'DOUGH'.

When the cycle has finished, transfer the dough to a floured surface and divide into 8 equal-sized pieces. Shape each piece into a sausage shape with tapered ends measuring approximately 23cm (9in) in length. Working with a piece at a time, join the ends together to make a circle, then pinch them gently to seal them. Place the circles on a lightly oiled baking sheet, leaving enough room between them for each to rise. Cover the circles with a sheet of oiled clingfilm and leave

them to prove for about 20 minutes.Preheat the oven to 200°C/400°F/GM 6. Bring a large pan of water to the boil, add the caster sugar and stir the water until the sugar has dissolved. Gently place 2 or 3 bagels in the boiling water and let them cook for 1 minute, turning once in the water, using a slotted spoon. Lift each bagel out of the water, gently shaking it as you do so to remove as much water as possible, before returning it to the baking tray. Repeat the process until all of the bagels have been cooked.

Beat the egg yolk with the water, then brush this mixture over each of the bagels.

Bake the bagels in the oven for 12 to 15 minutes, or until they are golden. Transfer the bagels to a wire rack and leave them to cool.

Ingredients
1 cup water, tepid
4 tablespoons butter, melted and cooled
1 tablespoon caster sugar
1 teaspoon salt
3 cups white-bread flour
1½ teaspoons yeast

To finish
25g (1oz) caster sugar
yolk of 1 egg
1 tablespoon water

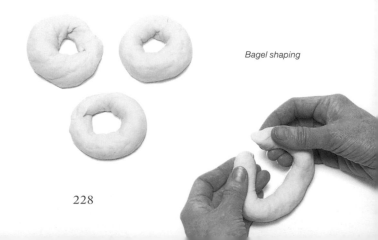

Bagel shaping

228

Bridge rolls

Preheat the oven to 220°/425°F /GM 7. When the rolls have almost doubled in size, remove the clingfilm and lightly brush the top of each with some milk. Now bake the rolls in the oven for 15 to 20 minutes, or until they are golden.

Remove the rolls from the oven, brush the top of each with some milk and then transfer them to a wire rack and cover them with a clean tea towel. (This will give them their distinctively soft, but slightly shiny, surface.) Leave the rolls to cool before serving them.

Ingredients
1 medium-sized egg, beaten
$^3/_4$ cup milk, warmed to a
    temperature of between
    21 and 28°C
1 tablespoon butter, melted
1 teaspoon caster sugar
$^1/_2$ teaspoon salt
2 cups white-bread flour
1 teaspoon yeast

To finish
a little milk for brushing
    over

Whisk the egg and milk together, then place the first seven ingredients in the baking pan. Set the programme to 'DOUGH'.

When the dough is ready, transfer it to a floured surface. Divide and shape the dough into 15 small, elongated-oval shapes, then place them on a greased baking tray, allowing enough room between them for each to rise. Cover the rolls with a piece of oiled clingfilm and leave them in a warm place to prove.

Shaping bridge rolls on tray

Seeded rolls

Seeded rolls in tray

Ingredients

$^1/_2$ cup water

3 tablespoons butter,
   melted and cooled

1 teaspoon caster sugar

$^1/_2$ teaspoon salt

1 cup white-bread flour

1 cup wholemeal-bread
   flour

1 teaspoon yeast

To finish

2 teaspoons sesame seeds

1 teaspoon fennel seeds

1 teaspoon cumin seeds

beaten egg for brushing
   over

Place the first seven ingredients in the baking pan. Set the programme to 'DOUGH'.

When the dough is ready, transfer it to a floured surface and knead it briefly. Divide the dough into 9 equal-sized pieces, then shape the pieces into balls. Place the balls in rows of three on a greased baking tin measuring 17.75cm (7in). Cover the balls with a piece of oiled clingfilm and leave them to prove in a warm place.

Preheat the oven to 220°C/425°F /GM 7. Place the sesame, fennel and cumin seeds in a small bowl and mix them together.

When the dough has almost doubled in size, remove the clingfilm, lightly brush the top of each roll with some beaten egg, then sprinkle over the seeds. Place the rolls in the oven and bake them for 15 to 20 minutes, or until they are golden. Transfer the rolls to a wire rack and leave them to cool before serving them.

232

Brioche buns

Shaping brioche

Ingredients

1 cup milk, warmed to a
    temperature of between
    21 and 28°C
1 teaspoon honey
1½ teaspoons yeast
3¼ cups white-bread flour
50g (2oz) butter, melted
    and cooled
2 eggs beaten
4 tablespoons caster sugar
pinch of salt

To finish
beaten egg for brushing
    over

Pour the warmed milk into a mixing bowl and then add the honey, yeast and a ³/₄ cup of white-bread flour. Mix the ingredients together, then cover the bowl with a sheet of clingfilm and leave the mixture to prove in a warm place for 1 to 2 hours.

When the mixture has risen and looks quite bubbly, pour it into the baking pan and add the rest of the white-bread flour, then the butter, eggs, caster sugar and salt. Set the programme to 'DOUGH'.

When the dough is ready, transfer it to a floured surface. Divide the dough into 16 pieces. Taking one piece at a time, pinch off a small piece of dough, about the size of your thumb tip, and then roll both pieces of dough into balls. Place the larger ball in a well-greased tartlet tin and press the smaller ball on top. Continue this procedure with the rest of the dough. Cover the dough with a piece of oiled clingfilm and leave it to rise. Preheat the oven to 220°C/425°F/GM 7. When the dough has almost doubled in size, remove the clingfilm, brush over some beaten egg and bake the buns in the oven for 5 minutes. Reduce the temperature to 180°C/350°F/GM 4 and continue to bake the buns for a further 10 minutes, or until they are golden. Transfer the buns to a wire rack and leave them to cool before serving them.

Soft, white floury baps

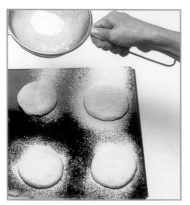

Flouring white baps on tray

Place the first seven ingredients in the baking pan in the order in which they are listed above. Set the programme to 'DOUGH'.

When the cycle has been completed, transfer the dough to a lightly floured surface and knead it briefly. Using your hands, shape the dough into a thick, short sausage shape and then, using a knife, cut it into 8 equal-sized slices. Using your hands, gently roll out each disc of dough until it is approximately 1.3cm (¹/₂in) thick and measures about 12.75cm (5in) across. Through a sieve, dust the top of each round with some flour, then cover the dough with a sheet of clingfilm and leave it in a warm place to rise (but not too warm a place

because the baps' texture benefits from a longer, slower rise).

Preheat the oven to 200°C/400°F /GM 6. When the baps have almost doubled in size, remove the clingfilm and sieve a little more flour over each of them. Bake the baps in the oven for 15 minutes, or until they are golden at the edges and have cooked through. Transfer the baps to a wire rack, cover them with a clean tea towel and leave them to cool.

To serve the baps, split them open and fill them with a filling of your choice.

Ingredients
¹/₂ cup water, tepid
¹/₂ cup milk, warmed
2 tablespoons butter, melted and cooled
1 teaspoon caster sugar
¹/₂ teaspoon salt
3 cups white-bread flour
¹/₂ teaspoon yeast

To finish
flour for dusting over

Croissants

Pour the tepid water into a large mixing bowl, then add the yeast, 1 teaspoon caster sugar and 1 cup of the flour. Stir the ingredients well to mix them together, then cover the bowl and leave it in a warm place for 2 to 3 hours.

Place the butter between 2 sheets of greaseproof paper and, using a rolling pin, roll it out until it forms a rough square approximately 5mm (¼in) thick. Now chill the butter.

When the yeast and flour mixture is ready (surface will be bubbly), transfer it to the baking pan and add the remaining flour, caster sugar and salt. Set the programme to 'DOUGH'.

When the cycle has been completed, transfer the dough to a well-floured surface and knead it briefly. Using a rolling pin, roll out the dough so that it is approximately 2.5cm (1in) wider than your sheet of butter and half as long again.

Unwrap the chilled butter and lay it on the dough, leaving a small border of dough on three sides at one end. Fold the remaining piece of dough over half of the butter,

then fold the remaining piece of butter and dough over it so that all of the butter has been enclosed within three layers of dough.

Using a rolling pin, press the edges together to seal them, then roll out the dough into an oblong that is three times as long as it is wide. Fold the top third of dough over the middle third, then bring up the bottom third so that you again have three layers. Give the dough a quarter turn and repeat the rolling-and-folding procedure once more. Place the dough on a lightly floured plate, cover it with a sheet of clingfilm and

Ingredients

1 cup water, tepid
1½ teaspoons yeast
1 teaspoon caster sugar
3 cups bread flour
3 tablespoons caster sugar
1 teaspoon salt

To finish

250g (9oz) unsalted butter, chilled
beaten egg

Folding up croissant

Just before croissant shaping

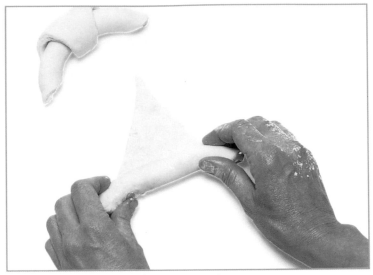

Forming croissant shape

chill it in the fridge for 30 minutes.

Repeat the rolling-and-folding process twice more, then chill the dough in the fridge for another 30 minutes.

Using a rolling pin, roll out the dough to a thickness of 5mm ($\frac{1}{4}$in). Trim the edges so that they are straight and then cut the dough into triangles that are taller than their base. Taking one triangle, roll it up from the base, curling in the ends slightly as you roll. Tuck under the tip and place the croissant on a lightly floured baking tray. Repeat the rolling process with all of the triangles, leaving space between each on the baking tray for them to rise. Loosely cover the croissants with a sheet of clingfilm and return them to the fridge

to chill for 30 minutes.

Preheat the oven to 200°C/400°F /GM 6. Brush the top of each croissant with some beaten egg and then bake them in the oven for 15 to 20 minutes, or until they have risen and turned golden. Transfer the croissants to a wire rack and leave them to cool.

Finishing croissant fold

Chocolate croissants

Folding butter and dough

Pour the water into a large mixing bowl, then add the yeast, 1 teaspoon of the caster sugar and 1 cup of the white-bread flour. Stir the ingredients until they are well mixed, then cover the bowl and leave it in a warm place for 2 to 3 hours.

Place the butter between 2 sheets of greaseproof paper and then, using a rolling pin, roll it out until it forms a rough square shape approximately 5mm ($^1/_4$in) thick. Now chill the butter.

Place the chocolate and cream in a bowl and set the bowl over a pan of simmering water. Stir the mixture constantly until the chocolate has melted, then set it to one side to cool.

When the yeast and flour mixture is ready (surface is bubbly), transfer it to the baking pan and add the remaining caster sugar, flour and salt. Set the programme to 'DOUGH'.

When the cycle has been completed, transfer the dough to a well-floured surface and knead it briefly. Using a rolling pin, roll out the dough so that it is approximately 2.5cm (1in) wider than your sheet of butter and half as long again.

Unwrap the chilled butter and lay it on the dough, leaving a small border of dough on three sides at one end. Fold the remaining piece of dough over half of the butter, then fold the remaining piece of butter and dough over it so that all of the butter has been enclosed within three layers of dough.

Making the first fold

Ingredients

1 cup water, tepid
1$^1/_2$ teaspoons yeast
4 teaspoons caster sugar
3 cups white-bread flour
$^1/_2$ teaspoon salt

To finish

250g (9oz) unsalted butter, chilled
150g (5oz) dark chocolate, broken into small pieces
3 tablespoons double cream
beaten egg

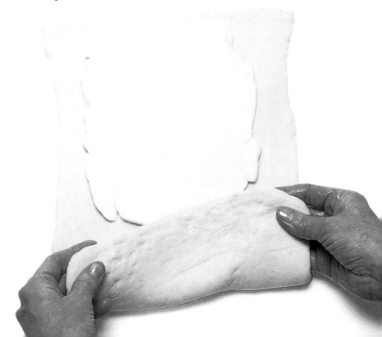

Using a rolling pin, press the edges together to seal them. Give the dough a quarter turn to the left (the completely enclosed edge should always be on the left), then roll out the dough into an oblong that is three times as long as it is wide. Fold the top third of dough over the middle third, then bring up the bottom third so that you again have three layers. Give the dough a quarter turn and repeat the rolling-and-folding procedure once more. Place the dough on a lightly floured plate, cover it with a sheet of clingfilm and chill it in the fridge for 30 minutes.

Repeat the rolling-and-folding process twice more, then chill the dough in the fridge for another 30 minutes.

Using a rolling pin, roll out the dough to a thickness of 5mm (¹⁄₄in), trim the edges so that they are straight and then cut the dough into 12 oblongs. Spread a generous teaspoon of the cooled chocolate mixture down the centre of each oblong, making sure that it doesn't quite reach the top and bottom edges. Now bring up

the sides so that the chocolate mixture is enclosed and pinch together the edges to seal them. Place the croissants, with the join underneath, on a lightly floured baking tray, leaving enough space between them for each to rise. Loosely cover the croissants with a sheet of clingfilm and return them to the fridge to chill for 30 minutes. Preheat the oven to 200°C/400°F /GM 6. Brush the top of each croissant with some beaten egg and then bake them in the oven for 15 to 20 minutes, or until they have risen and have turned golden. Transfer the croissants to a wire rack and leave them to cool.

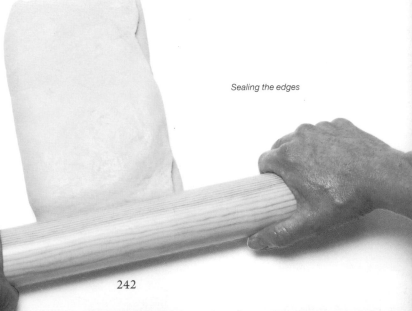

Sealing the edges

Chelsea buns

Rolling Chelsea buns

Ingredients
$^1/_2$ cup water, tepid
$^1/_2$ cup milk, warmed to a
  temperature of between
  21 and 28°C
1 medium-sized egg, beaten
75g (3oz) butter, melted
  and cooled
3 tablespoons caster sugar
$^1/_2$ teaspoon salt
$3^1/_2$ cups white-bread flour
2 teaspoons yeast

To finish
50g (2oz) butter, melted
  and cooled
100g ($3^1/_2$oz) raisins
50g (2oz) mixed peel
4 tablespoons caster sugar
milk for brushing over

Place the first eight ingredients in the baking pan. Set the programme to 'DOUGH'.

When the dough is ready, transfer it to a floured surface and knead it briefly. Using a rolling pin, roll out the dough into an oblong measuring approximately 35.5 x 23cm (14 x 9in). Liberally brush the melted butter over the surface of the dough, but not quite to the edges. Sprinkle over the raisins and mixed peel, along with 3 tablespoons of the caster sugar.

Taking one of the long edges, roll up the dough so that the filling is enclosed, then pinch the long edge to seal it. Using a sharp, dampened knife, cut the dough into 16 equal-sized slices. Place each piece, cut side up, on a well-buttered baking tin 23cm (9in) square. Cover the dough with a piece of oiled clingfilm and leave the dough to prove in a warm place.

Preheat the oven to 220°C/425°F /GM 7. When the dough has almost doubled in size, remove the clingfilm, lightly brush the top of each roll with some milk and sprinkle over the remaining caster sugar. Bake the buns in the oven for 15 to 20 minutes, or until they are golden. Transfer the buns to a wire rack and leave them to cool before serving them.

245

Pretzels

Ingredients

$^2/_3$ cup water, tepid
1 teaspoon clear honey
1 teaspoon salt
2 cups white-bread flour
$^3/_4$ teaspoon yeast

To finish

yolk of 1 egg
1 tablespoon water, tepid
2–3 tablespoons sea salt

Place the first five ingredients in the baking pan in the order in which they are listed above. Set the programme to 'DOUGH'.

When the cycle has finished, transfer the dough to a floured surface and divide it into 12 equal-sized pieces. Using your hands, roll each piece into a sausage shape measuring approximately 30cm (12in) in length. Shape each length of dough into a pretzel shape by forming the central portion into a circle, crossing over the two end pieces where they meet and then laying them back over the circle so the ends just extend beyond it. Place the pretzels on a lightly oiled baking sheet and cover them with a piece of oiled clingfilm. Leave them to prove until they have almost doubled in size.

Preheat the oven to 200°C/400°F /GM 6. Beat the egg yolk with the water and brush the mixture over the pretzels. Sprinkle over the salt, then bake the pretzels in the oven for 15 minutes, or until they are dark golden. Transfer the pretzels to a wire rack and leave them to cool.

Shaping pretzel

Wholemeal grissini

Adding wholemeal flour

Place the ingredients in the baking pan in the order in which they are listed above. Set the programme to 'DOUGH'.

Preheat the oven to 220°C/425°F/GM 7.

When the cycle has been completed, transfer the dough to a floured surface and knead it for 2 to 3 minutes. Pinch off around 40 pieces of the dough. Working one at a time, roll and stretch each piece into a long round roughly the thickness of a pencil and about 25.5cm (10in) in length. As you complete them, place each round on a lightly oiled baking sheet, leaving a little space between each for them to rise, and cover them with a sheet of oiled clingfilm while you shape the remaining pieces of dough.

The pieces do not need to rise for a second time, so when you have shaped all of them, bake them in the oven for 10 minutes, or until they are golden and very crisp (they should easily snap in two and should not be 'doughy' inside). Transfer the grissini to a wire rack and leave them to cool.

These grissini make good snacks just as they are, but you could also serve them with dips.

Ingredients
$^2/_3$ cup water, tepid
1 tablespoon olive oil
1 teaspoon salt
$1^1/_2$ cups white-bread flour
$1^1/_2$ cups wholemeal-bread flour
$^1/_2$ teaspoon yeast

Rolling grissini

Fig, orange and almond rolls

Putting rolls into tin

Whisk together the egg and milk, then place the first eight ingredients in the baking pan. Set the programme to 'DOUGH'.

In a mixing bowl, combine the figs, orange zest and honey.

When the dough is ready, transfer it to a floured surface and knead it briefly. Using a rolling pin, roll out the dough into an oblong measuring approximately 30.5 x 23cm (12 x 9in). Sprinkle the fig mixture over the dough.

Taking one of the long edges, roll up the dough as you would a swiss roll. Now turn the dough so that the seam is resting on the work surface. Using a knife, cut the dough into 12 equal-sized slices and then place each slice, cut side facing upwards, in a deep, well-greased muffin tin. Loosely cover the dough with a piece of oiled clingfilm and leave it to prove in a warm place.

Preheat the oven to 220°/425°F /GM 7. In a small pan, gently heat the butter and sugar until the sugar has dissolved, then set the pan to one side.

When the dough has almost doubled in size, remove the clingfilm, lightly brush the top of each roll with the butter-and-sugar glaze and then cook the rolls in the oven for 15 to 20 minutes, or until they are golden. Transfer the rolls to a wire rack and leave them to cool.

Adding melted butter

Ingredients

1 medium-sized egg, beaten
¾ cup milk, warmed to a temperature of between 21 and 28°C
1 tablespoon butter, melted and cooled
1 teaspoon caster sugar
½ teaspoon salt
3 cups white-bread flour
½ cup ground almonds
1 teaspoon yeast

To finish

150g (5oz) dried, ready-to-eat figs, roughly chopped
freshly grated zest of 1 orange
1 tablespoon honey
2 tablespoons butter, melted
1 tablespoon caster sugar

I would like to thank Morphy Richards for the loan of the Bread machines which worked almost non-stop to produce this book.

Thanks also to Emily Taylor at Saffron, Paul Forrester, Colin Bowling and Laura Forrester.

I must also thank family and friends for their taste testing, comments and inspiration.

And lastly to my mother.